FUNERAL
MEDITATIONS

FUNERAL MEDITATIONS

William R. Baird, Sr. *and*
John E. Baird

Nashville ABINGDON PRESS *New York*

FUNERAL MEDITATIONS

Copyright © 1966 by Abingdon Press

Library of Congress Catalog Card Number: 66-14990

CONTENTS

INTRODUCTION

The meditations that follow are written out of the conviction that the Bible should be the center and focus of the funeral service. Other matters certainly have a place. A service of worship would seem unnecessarily limited without music, prayers, and the rich resources to be found in secular literature. Some specific mention should be made of the departed, although the extended eulogy is both unnecessary and out of place. However, all these things would be empty and meaningless apart from the Christian hope, which rests upon the good news of what God has done for us in Christ.

Let attention be centered on the precious promises of the gospel. These bring comfort to the sorrowing. They turn attention from the loss that has been suffered to the eternal truths of our Christian faith. They deliver the preacher from the necessity of passing judgment, whether favorable or unfavorable, upon the dead. They deepen the understanding of even the most casual visitor to the service.

The funeral may begin with the minister's announcement of the purpose of the assembly. Words such as the following would be appropriate:

My friends, we are gathered today for three purposes. First, we come to pay tribute in friendship and love to one who was dear to all of us. This is not a "last" tribute, for the most beautiful memorial left by anyone is not carved on stone, not even in a service such as this. It is the memorial left in the hearts of those who knew and loved him. Then, we come to offer our sympathy to these loved ones who are in sorrow this day. Finally, we come to find words of comfort and strength from the Word of God.

The following plan for the memorial service would be a simple, yet beautiful procedure:
1. Appropriate music from instrument, soloist, or church congregation.
2. The minister's statement of the purpose of the service.
3. A prayer expressing adoration for the God who rules over both life and death, thanksgiving for the hopes and promises of the gospel, and petition for the strengthening of faith in this difficult time.
4. A brief obituary giving the central facts of the life of the deceased and the names of the close members of the family.
5. The reading of a brief passage of scripture.
6. The funeral meditation.
7. A prayer of thanksgiving for the fine example set for us by those who have gone before, of petition for strength for those left behind, and of dedication and submission of all those present to the supreme will of the Almighty.
8. Other appropriate music.

This entire service should be very brief, taking not more than fifteen or twenty minutes from beginning to end.

Only a few minutes are needed to pay proper tribute and to bring a measure of comfort. To spend more time than this is to impose an undeserved cruelty upon those in sorrow.

Those who examine the meditations given here will discover that they are not evangelistic sermons. The funeral service is not the time to preach the departed into heaven or into hell. Whatever his life may have been, he is beyond the reach of the minister's words. Neither is this service the time to convert the members of his family. The ethics of attempting to do so would be very questionable. People in sorrow and under the emotional stress of grief are not able to make the kind of decision that conversion involves. To attempt to force them to do so in the funeral service indicates a lack of respect for them as human beings. The preacher has a right to point to the promises of the gospel at such a time. He has no right to judge the departed, and he has no right to demand a decision from those left behind.

These meditations are not offered with the thought that they should be read, exactly as given, for any particular service. The minister will want to change and adapt each one to suit the individual service which he will conduct. These talks are offered as guides to help the minister in choosing the most appropriate scripture and in discussing it in a manner which will be most helpful and meaningful to those attending the service.

Each minister must also plan a brief service for the graveside. Many Protestants will probably wish to avoid the formal words of committal. The following procedure could be used instead:

11

1. A passage of scripture such as II Cor. 5:1; John 11: 25; I Cor. 15:21-22.
2. A brief poem of comfort such as Tennyson's "Crossing the Bar," or Robert Freeman's "In My Father's House." The entire twenty-third psalm may be repeated in place of scripture verse and poem.
3. A short prayer including some expression of committal such as: "We have done all that loving hands can do. We commit this mortal body to the ground, but we rest in the assurance that our friend is in thy hands."
4. A benediction such as the priestly one found in Num. 6:24-26.
5. A concluding statement: "On behalf of the family, I wish to express their appreciation to all of you, their friends, for coming to the service, for your kind words and thoughts of sympathy, and for all the beautiful flowers. God bless you all. This concludes our service."

May each one who reads the following pages find his own faith renewed and his desire to comfort the sorrowing strengthened, in the name of him who is the Source of all strength and comfort.

1

With Untroubled Hearts

John 14:1-7

"Let not your hearts be troubled," Jesus commanded his disciples a few hours before his death. He might have told them not to be sorrowful, but our Lord did not command the impossible. When face to face with separation and loss, all men are conscious of their sorrow. Even Jesus, aware of the resurrection power that was his, shed tears beside the tomb of his friend Lazarus. Being sorrowful at death is not forbidden, even for the Christian. The command to the disciples and to us is that we are not to be troubled.

What are the reasons for this command? Why should we not be anxious and worried in the face of death, this last great enemy? Why should we not be disturbed at the unknown void which marks the end for us all?

Jesus gave three answers on that night long ago. First, we are to believe in God. Surely, the Eternal, the Creator, the Omnipotent would never be blocked by the event that we call death. We place a dry seed in the moist soil, and it apparently dies and decays. Yet from that very seed springs the life which blossoms forth into the beautiful flower. The changing seasons move from the cold death of winter to the green birth of spring each year, thus bearing witness to God's power to bring life from death. The God who created all the beauties of the heavens and the earth, who brought forth life as the crown of creation, will not let that life be wasted and brought to nothing.

Our Heavenly Father does care about his creation. He numbers each hair of each head. He clothes the lily of the field which blooms today and is destroyed tomorrow. He knows when even a sparrow falls from the heavens. How much more, then, does he care about us, his children, in these moments of sorrow?

Moreover, the God whom we call Father loves us far beyond anything else in his creation. We read in the Scriptures that he loved us enough to give his only begotten Son, that through faith in him we need not perish but may find eternal life. (John 3:16.) Let not your hearts be troubled, then, at times such as these. You believe in God.

Let not your hearts be troubled, for you believe also in Christ. Know him as the one who shared our moments of temptation, our moments of suffering, our moments of sorrow. See him as he goes to visit the two sisters in Bethany, to console them at the loss of their brother. Watch him as the tears of sympathy fill his eyes. But hear the calm assurance in his voice as he tells the sorrowing sisters, "I am the resurrection, and the life" (John 11:25). Hear him as he calls, "Lazarus, come forth!" and he who was dead comes out of the tomb. And join our Lord's followers in the garden that first Easter morning as they find the stone rolled back, the grave empty, and the Christ walking among them. Hear them shout the Easter message: "He is not here! He is risen! Don't seek the living among the dead." (Luke 24:5.) "He is the first fruits of them that sleep." (I Cor. 15:20.) Let not your hearts be troubled; believe in him.

"Let not your hearts be troubled," Jesus told them. Believe in the Father; believe in the Son. But beyond this faith, we are asked to believe in a place, the place that our Lord has prepared for those who love him. In his Father's house are many mansions, many dwelling places, many rooms. He goes to prepare this place for us.

"What will the place be like?" we ask. We are foolish to ask, as if our minds could understand these things. As well might a caterpillar ask about the life of the butterfly, or the acorn about the oak tree. Still, the Bible gives us some hints. Christ prepares a place for us where sin and sorrow and death will be unknown, where we will be reunited with the loved ones who have gone before us, never to be separated again. He prepares a place for us which will truly be "home."

Many of us have had the experience of living far from our families as our work takes us to distant places. We long to be with parents and with brothers and sisters, but it is impossible for us to do so. Letters and occasional telephone calls make poor substitutes.

Then the day comes, perhaps in the summertime, when we take a vacation from our duties and finally have the leisure to make that trip home. We look forward eagerly to the day of departure. Before long we are counting the hours and then counting the miles that separate us from our destination. Finally, the moment arrives. The old family home is there before us, and Mother and Dad come

15

rushing out to greet us before we even have the chance to get out of the car. Such a joyous reunion takes place as the family is united once more!

Death may be regarded as a journey of a similar nature. Those we love have gone on, and we are separated from them. Finally, the call comes to us as well, and we make that long journey into eternity. There, at our destination, we find the warm smiles and the welcoming arms of those we have loved. For all eternity the family will be complete, never to be separated again.

Even in your sorrow, let not your heart be troubled. Believe in the Father. Believe also in the Son. Know the reality of that moment, coming soon for all of us, when we shall all be together as children in the Father's house.

Lord, strengthen our faith that we may not be troubled about these things which we cannot understand. Grant that we may live in the hope and comfort which spring from our knowledge of thy love; through Jesus Christ, our Lord. Amen.

2

Things We Like About Death

Hebrews 9:27

We naturally think of death as a sad experience, and there are many things we do not like about this final parting. We look with dread upon the suffering that often heralds its coming. We think of the separation, of the sad farewell which death always involves as one is taken from us and we are left alone. We always fear the unknown, and we know very little about death. Our loved ones go and do not return again to tell us where they are or what their experience has been.

Since we are also Christians, our sadness leaves us troubled in mind and conscience. We, of all people, should know the reality of the human hope of life beyond the grave. We may be sad and lonely at these moments of parting, but our sadness should never overcome us. We see death from a different perspective than does the rest of mankind. Rather than giving way to our sorrow or cursing the fate that awaits us, let us notice a different aspect to death, some of the ways in which it fits into the great plan of God for our good.

Death is an appointment made for us by God. As such,

it has a certain beauty that we should not overlook. The flowers which we bring as a tribute to the departed should remind us of this fact. We know that before each flower could come into being, a little seed or bulb had to be planted in the ground to die. The seed or bulb has no beauty; the beauty is in the flower. The seed is the means by which the flower comes into being. Thus the act by which the gardener trusts the seed to the ground, in anticipation of the flower which will grow, is a beautiful act, a work of faith and hope.

If God has a plan for the seed, he must also have a plan for the human being whom he created in his own likeness. Man is of more importance than a flower. We are taught that our Heavenly Father knows all things, that he knows when even the smallest sparrow falls from the sky. Can we not trust him to make provision for man? We watch the fruit tree as it seems to die in the autumn, its leaves falling to the ground. But that death is only a prelude to the buds and blossoms and fruit of the spring that follows. What we call death must be something like the same process. It is all we can see of the transformation of man into that beautiful existence beyond. It is the prelude to that life for which man was created from the beginning of his creation. Let some of the beauty of this life which God has prepared for us, then, touch also the experience of death.

In faith, we can appreciate not only the beauty of death, but also its universality. It is appointed unto man to die. If our Lord tarry, there are no exceptions. Would we want the plan to be otherwise? Suppose that some were to die and others remain. Then the parting would be sorrowful indeed, for there would be no hope of a reunion. Homes would be broken forever. Of course, we cannot bring our loved ones back from the grave. If we think of the pain and sorrow and suffering of this life, it often seems pure selfishness that we would want to do so. But in the great plan of God, we all go, sooner or later, to meet them where they are.

Death stands at the end of life like a great doorway through which we all must pass. We cannot see through it, and the shadows that block our vision on the other side sometimes seem fearsome to us. Yet, as Christians, we know that our loved ones wait for us on the other side of the door. The time is short until, in the wisdom of God, the call comes to all of us to step through the doorway. Then how joyous the reunion in the Father's house!

Finally, we notice the pictures of death which are found in the Bible, descriptions far removed from the gloom that most of us feel at the word. The psalmist speaks of death as a shadowed valley through which we must pass. However, the Lord walks with us, and the valley is only a part of the road that leads to his house. There the table is spread, and we are received as welcome guests. (Ps. 23.) The apostle wrote of death as the time of departure, as though he were leaving on a journey. But the journey was made in order to receive a prize, a crown of righteousness which the Lord would award to him. (II Tim. 4:6-8.) The writer John, in the first of his three letters in our New Testament, saw death as a translation, a change from our present state into the very image of the Lord, for we see him and become like him. (I John 3:1-2.) How glorious are the promises the Bible makes about this experience which we fear so much!

One day a father came to Jesus, terribly concerned at the serious illness of his twelve-year-old daughter. In response to his plea, Jesus went with him toward the house where the girl lay ill. (Luke 8:41-56.) But the crowds were thick in the streets, and a woman stopped the Lord in order that she, too, might be healed. Before Jesus could get to the home of Jairus, a messenger came. "There is no point in disturbing the Teacher further. The girl is dead."

Jesus spoke words of hope to the sorrowing father. He took his close followers with him and walked through the jeering crowd of those who could see death only as the end of all things. He put them out of the house, substituting for their wailing his own quiet affirmation: not dead, but asleep. Then he took Jairus' daughter by the hand and said, "Little girl, get up now." As if waking from a nap, she got up and walked to the arms of her father and mother, healed and restored to them.

Here is a picture of death as the Christian sees it. Our loved ones are not dead, but asleep. At the hand of the Lord they arise, reunited with friends and family to be forever with the Lord.

Our Father, let the voice of faith speak to us in this, our hour of sorrow and need. Help us to see death, not as man sees it, but through the eyes of the one we know as the Resurrection and the Life; for in his name we pray. Amen.

3

Companionship in Death

Psalm 23

"The Lord is my Shepherd." We wonder when David wrote these words. Perhaps it was as a youth when he sat on the Judean hillside looking over his sheep. If so, this is a psalm of faith. This young man knew firsthand the shepherd's concern for the safety and welfare of his sheep. He had defended them against the attacks of the lion and the bear. He trusted that God loved him and would, in like manner, defend him against all enemies.

Perhaps the psalm was written later in life, after David had become king of Israel. It would remain a psalm of faith under these circumstances, but of faith plus experience. Now David knew the extent of his own sin and failure. He knew how little he deserved the protecting care of God. And yet, through all the tragic experiences of life, he had found these words to be true: "The Lord is my Shepherd; I shall not want."

Can we realize this same faith in our own experience as we face the great questions of life? We know that we must live, we must die, and we must move into eternity. Our sense of comfort and assurance would be so much greater

21

if we just knew that God cared for us throughout it all. The psalm gives us our answer. The Lord is our Shepherd; we shall lack for nothing throughout life, death, and the life beyond.

First, we see how God provides for us in life. He makes us to lie down in green pastures; that is, he provides the food we need to live. He leads us beside still waters, for it is only from the quiet pools that the sheep can drink. Besides providing these necessities for the body, he gives restoration for the soul in those times when discouragement and despondency come upon us. He guides us in the paths of righteousness, showing us what is good, quickening our consciences, and strengthening us in moments of temptation.

Jesus taught us of such a God. Our Lord commanded that we are not to be anxious about food or drink or clothing. Our Heavenly Father provides all these things. He knows what we need before we even ask him. He clothes the lily of the field and provides food for the birds of the heaven. Yet he considers man far more important and precious than these objects of nature. Why should our faith be so small and our worries so large? The God who takes care of all these other things will surely take care of us. The Lord is our Shepherd; we shall not want.

The care of the Heavenly Father does not end when we come to the close of this life. Whatever makes us fear that it will? Can God somehow stop loving the man he created in his own image? Thus the psalmist goes on: "Yea, though I walk through the valley of the shadow of death, I shall fear no evil, for thou art with me." In these words he faces the real fact of death squarely. It is certainly a dark valley, deep

22

and terrible in its aspect. The shadows gather there, and we cannot see. The road does not seem to be marked, and no travelers come back to tell us the way. The psalmist faces all these facts and then adds the one affirmation that changes everything: "For thou art with me." Here is the reason we need fear no evil; God walks beside us. Here is the basis for our confidence that we walk *through* the valley; we don't stop there. Our Shepherd leads us through, and he knows the way.

We admire David for his confidence and faith. As a youth, he could think of the God who cared for him as he cared for the sheep and led them through the difficult places. As a man, he could witness to his own experience. God always walked with him, even in the face of death. But our faith can be far richer than David's. It is founded on the one who came to us as the Resurrection and the Life, who was crucified, dead, and buried, and rose again on the third day. We said that no traveler has come back from the valley of the shadow of death to tell us the way, but that statement is not quite true. One traveler did come back. And when we must walk through the valley ourselves, we can know that he walks with us and leads us through. In the moment of death, the Lord is our Shepherd. We shall not want.

But what lies beyond this valley? Does the care of our Father extend to eternity? To ask the question is to answer it. The psalmist pictures a traveler who has arrived at his destination. The dangers and hardships of the journey are past. Now he is home, in his Father's house. The table is spread before him with all manner of good things for him to eat. His cup is filled and filled again until every thirst is

23

satisfied. His wandering is over; now he is home to stay. His head is anointed as his Father delights to honor him. He has known goodness and kindness from time to time; now he enjoys these things constantly as he lives forever in his Father's home.

These things are not some peculiar, happy dream of a shepherd boy. The writer of the Revelation heard the Spirit of God crying that blessed or happy are the dead who die in the Lord. They rest from their labors, and their good deeds follow after them. (Rev. 14:13.) Jesus spoke of a place prepared for us, of the many rooms in his Father's house that would be ready to receive us when we go to dwell therein. (John 14:2-3.)

Kipling's words are fanciful, but they picture a divine truth:

When Earth's last picture is painted, and the tubes are
  twisted and dried,
When the oldest colors have faded, and the youngest critic
  has died,
We shall rest, and—faith, we shall need it—lie down for an
  aeon or two,
Till the Master of All Good Workmen shall set us to work anew!

And those that were good shall be happy: they shall sit in
  a golden chair;
They shall splash at a ten-league canvas with brushes of
  comets' hair;
They shall find real saints to draw from—Magdalene, Peter,
  and Paul;
They shall work for an age at a sitting, and never be tired
  at all!

And only the Master shall praise us, and only the Master
  shall blame;
And no one shall work for money, and no one shall work for
  fame;
But each for the joy of the working, and each, in his
  separate star
Shall draw the Thing as he sees It for the God of Things
  as They are! [1]

The Lord is our Shepherd; we shall not want. In life,
in death, in eternity, God provides for our needs, according
to his riches in glory in Christ Jesus. (Phil. 4:19.)

*Our Father, we look to thee as sheep looking to the good
shepherd. We know that thou hast always provided for us
in days past. Give us the faith to trust thee, even unto death
and beyond; through Jesus Christ our Lord. Amen.*

[1] Rudyard Kipling, "L'envoi." From *Rudyard Kipling's Verse: Definitive Edition.* Reprinted by permission of Mrs. George Bambridge and Doubleday & Company, Inc.

4

The Beauty of Death

Ecclesiastes 3:11

Life seems to be a mixture of the good and the bad, of love and hatred, of joy and sorrow. Some law of compensation seems to operate so that everything we like is balanced by something we dislike. When things seem to go well for us, we become fearful about what may happen next; our good luck must be matched by an equal amount of misfortune. Sometimes we even think of God as taking care of the good and the Devil as taking care of the evil, and we wonder whether God is strong enough to win in the long run.

In the midst of our doubts, we hear this promise of the ancient writer: God makes everything beautiful in its time. This proposition is one we would like to believe. It implies that good is more powerful than evil. It even indicates that suffering and sorrow, pain and sin have no real existence at all. These things are only temporary. They may seem overwhelming at times, but we are limited in our outlook. Things seem ugly and painful to us because we see them only half done and even twisted from the purpose for which God intended them. If we could only see things whole and completed and properly used, we would be able to grasp their true beauty. The promise is that eventually we will be given the proper perspective to view things as they truly are. God makes everything beautiful in its time.

The principle does seem to operate in nature. Consider the seed as an example. To us it seems dry and ugly, a shriveled and lifeless thing. Can you imagine a person bringing a packet of seeds in memory of a departed loved one? And yet, the seed does contain within itself all the beauty of the flower. In the orderly processes of nature, the seed puts forth the shoot, the shoot becomes the plant, the plant bears the bud, and the bud breaks open into glorious blossom. Then man comes, recognizing in his tardy fashion the beauty that was there all along, gathers the blossoms, and puts them on display to remind himself that God does, indeed, make all things beautiful in their time.

Notice the beauty in the ever changing, ever alike cycle of our seasons. We naturally enjoy the beauty of the springtime. The warm sun makes us forget the discomforts of winter, and all nature seems to throb with returning life. Flowers appear, and the fruit trees adorn themselves with blossoms. The soft rains spread our hillsides with green. But is the summer any less beautiful? Now the fields are golden with the ripening grain, and the trees hang heavy with their fruit. White clouds drift through the burnished blue sky, and the lazy streams reflect the warm sun. Our ears catch the drone of a bumblebee and the song of the meadowlark, and we wonder if any time of year can compare with summer.

Then the season moves on to autumn. The trees dress themselves in scarlet and gold. The yellow pumpkins lie fat against the brown earth. Walnuts loose their hold on the branches, fall to the ground, break out of their green hulls, and lie brown and moist among the leaves. The long lines of geese honk faintly as they follow their leader southward. Our hearts respond to these changes by turning to God in humble thanksgiving, and fall seems the most beautiful season of all. But then the snow comes, and the countryside is wrapped in sparkling white. Every tree seems trimmed with cotton, and every roof wears a diamond necklace of ice that breaks the sunlight into all the colors of the spectrum. Even the wind seems frozen, and the smoke rises in a straight, gray column from each chimney. Which season is best? Each part of the year has its own beauty; how can we really compare them? Let us agree only that God makes all things beautiful in their time.

The same principle may be seen in human life. Which of the ages of mankind is most beautiful? We think immediately of the dimpled smile of the tiny babe in all her helplessness and innocence and answer that this must be the most beautiful time. But that image is replaced by the schoolgirl with hair in pigtails and braces on her teeth as she runs down the front walk and throws her arms around her Daddy's neck to welcome him home from work. Or we see the same young lady, grown now, dressed in academic cap and gown, as she moves across the stage to receive her college diploma. Even this beauty is overshadowed a short time later as she stands slim and radiant at the altar, speaking in a low, clear voice to pledge her love to the man of her dreams. Time moves on again, and we see the beauty of love in the face of a new mother as she looks into the eyes of her firstborn son. Which age is more beautiful? Look into the face of the same woman as the years move past.

The golden hair is white now. The face is no longer smooth, but the lines drawn there have been inscribed by love. Her beauty is not a characteristic of outward appearance but of inner character, of a joy and hope in life that seem to shine through every feature. Each age seems to offer a greater beauty than the age before. God makes all things beautiful in their time.

Some may object that we have been thinking about ideals and not realities. Not all flowers are beautiful, and some seeds never grow at all. Many lives have been twisted and warped until no beauty is apparent in them. We cannot overlook these facts. However, we direct our attention to another scene. One day, long ago, an ugly cross was raised on the outskirts of an ancient city. Upon that instrument of torture was nailed the mangled body of a young prophet who had been stripped and beaten, cursed and spat upon. A crown woven of thorn branches was crushed down upon his head, and a sarcastic inscription placed above him. This was the king of the Jews. Could anything change such a picture into a thing of beauty?

But three days later the tomb was empty. God made him both Lord and Christ, this Jesus who was crucified. Today, lives are devoted in humble and loving service in the name of this same Jesus. Even his cross has become a thing of beauty, worn as jewelry or even given the central place in our greatest cathedrals. God makes all things beautiful in their time.

Our faith in this promise gives us hope, even in the time of death. God still rules in all the affairs of men. He is the weaver; we are but threads in his pattern. One of our loved ones is taken from us, and we feel that the whole design has been spoiled because that thread is gone. Our problem is that we always watch the weaving from beneath, from the wrong side of the cloth. God weaves from above, with the true pattern spread before him. In his wisdom he takes one thread through the cloth and brings it out on the upper side, that his design may be beautiful and complete. God makes all things beautiful in their time.

Our Father, in the moment of sorrow we confess our lack of understanding. Thy ways are so far above ours, and we cannot see. Remind us of thy power and thy love. Give us the faith to trust beyond our sight; through Jesus Christ our Lord. Amen.

5

A Glorious Awakening

John 11:11

If anyone could understand the nature of death, surely Jesus Christ was the one. He followed the will of his Father in perfect obedience. He constantly viewed all life from the vantage point of eternity. He came to reveal God to us. Naturally, we expect him to have something to say about this last great event which marks the close of life on earth for each of us.

In several places the New Testament records comments that Jesus made about death. Perhaps none of these is kinder in tone and more helpful in sympathy than the one we have just read. These are the words Jesus spoke upon learning of the death of a beloved companion: "Our friend Lazarus is asleep." Even in modern times we are faithful to these words, for we place our loved ones in the tomb reclining as if in sleep. Jesus, however, did not speak idle language to create beautiful poetry. His words expressed a profound truth; and if our Lord saw death as sleep, we can learn to see it in the same way.

Sleep is a perfectly natural part of our existence. We do not fear these moments of rest; in fact, we often need them and wish for them. Sleep may break our contact with reality for a time, but we know the morning will follow. We awaken with renewed strength for the challenges of a new day. In such respects death is just like sleep. Why should we be any more afraid of the close of life's day than we are of every approaching sunset?

Of course, sleep and death are not quite identical. Some may feel that the differences between the two give rise to the sorrow, concern, and uncertainty that we feel as we face death. Let us, then, examine some of these differences in the light of our Christian faith. Perhaps a better understanding of what death really is will reduce the worry that we feel about our loved ones and ourselves.

When we fall asleep at night, we naturally expect to wake up in the same place in the morning. We would be surprised to wake up in a different room, in a different town, or even in a different kind of existence entirely. In death, we experience this transition from one kind of life to the next. But our surprise is one of joy, for we awake to a kind of life so far different from ours that we can scarcely comprehend it now. The Bible tells us that we shall be where Jesus is, in a place he prepared for us, and that we shall be like him. (John 14; I John 3:2.)

In this life we wake in the morning with the same bodies in which we went to sleep at night. We may feel a bit better because of the rest, but we experience no basic change. If we were weak at night, we are weak also in the morning. The dawn may return us to a consciousness of the same pains that tortured us the night before. We experience hunger, thirst, and disease. Only the sleep of death really changes these things. Then we shall awake in a new and glorified body, a resurrection body. The weakness and pain, hunger and disease are things of the past. Our mortal bodies decay and are gone. They are of the dust and the earth, and to the earth they return. We are given immortal bodies, of the heavens rather than of the earth, made in the image of our Lord. (II Cor. 5:1.)

Each morning we wake up with the same problems that troubled us the night before. We appreciate the brief release sleep gives us from worries, but our relief is all too short. The morning comes when we must again pick up our burdens and face the new day with all its uncertainties. The sleep of death is a different thing, for in that brief night our problems all disappear. Most of the things we worried about here will seem so silly and inconsequential over there. Our knowledge here is so partial. There, we shall understand completely, even as God completely understands us. (I Cor. 13:12.)

Finally, our waking each morning finds us in the company of the same people who were with us the night before. We are happy, of course, to have those we love around us. At the same time, we are aware of those who are missing. Some have moved away, and the bonds of love seem broken by the distance. Others have been separated by enmity or misunderstanding. Still others seem gone forever, for Mother or Dad, son or daughter, brother or sister have passed on and are no longer here. We may dream of them at night, but they are still gone when we wake up in the morning.

The sleep of death is not the same. Then we wake to find ourselves surrounded by those we have loved and lost. We have come home, and all the members of the family soon gather there. Our misunderstandings are all made

33

clear. Those from far away seem always present. Mother, Dad, son, daughter, brother, and sister have their appointed places in our Heavenly Father's house. Forever we shall always be with the Lord.

Our friend Lazarus is asleep. Our Lord, who is the Resurrection and the Life, comes to waken him from that sleep. Each night we have, in some measure, a bit of this same experience. Death should hold no more terrors for us than our nights of rest, and it promises us so much more. With this understanding, we look forward to the great day when we all awake in the home prepared for us.

Our Father, we give thanks for the rest that thou hast provided for our physical bodies. Help us to understand death as the sleep that translates us and renews us, and reunites us with those we love and with thee. Give us a foretaste even now of the new life thou hast in store for us; through Jesus Christ our Lord. Amen.

6

On Birth and Death

Ecclesiastes 7:1

Our days are not all alike. As the evening comes and we look back over the experiences of the past hours, we realize how different these periods of time can seem to us. At times we relax at the close of the day with the feeling of work well done, of goals attained, of problems solved. These are the "good" days. At other times the evening finds us disappointed and frustrated with the manner in which the time has gone. We think of these as the "bad" days. Our hope is that the "good" may always exceed the "bad."

We think of the day of birth as one of the best days of all. A whole family may join in rejoicing that a child has been born. Gifts are showered upon the mother, and the father receives happy congratulations. Both parents begin to look forward in eager anticipation, to make plans for the future of the child who has joined the family.

The day of death is another time entirely. Now the smiles are turned to tears. We dress in black, speak in whispers, and seek to offer consolation to those who have suffered the loss of a loved one. Given a chance, all of us would avoid the day of death. Nevertheless, in spite of all these considerations, the Scripture tells us that the day of death is somehow better than the day of birth.

How can the writer make such a preposterous statement as this? We rebel at the foolishness of it. And yet, the more we think about death, the more we realize that the day of death is, in fact, a day of birth. It is a time of transition from one world to the next. It is leaving one kind of existence and moving to another. The difference between birth and death is a difference of viewpoint, not a difference of the events themselves. We see birth from the view of the world which is being entered. We welcome the new child to the home, the family, and the community. We see death, however, from the view of the world that is being left. We mourn the loss, the separation, and the broken fellowship. Somewhere, however, we can imagine the new world which our loved one has entered. There he has come into a new family, a new fellowship. Ties that had once been broken are being renewed. A heavenly family is being enlarged, and a new circle of love is being established. When seen from God's viewpoint, the day of death may indeed be better than the day of birth.

The day of death is better, for it leads all of us to serious thoughts about eternal things. The day of birth lends itself to foolish and idle dreams, the hopes of proud parents that probably have little basis in reality. The day of death reminds us all that life is such a short period compared to all eternity. So many of the things that occupy our time are of such little importance. Our amusements seem so vital until we ask ourselves what they really mean in the light of eternity. The treasures that we accumulate seem so precious until we take stock of the treasure we have laid up in heaven, where moth and rust won't consume and thieves won't break in to steal. Our troubles and worries seem to overwhelm us until we understand how small and temporary and even selfish they are. The day of death is a day of insight and self-evaluation. We stand at the graveside of our loved ones and realize that there, but for the grace of God, we ourselves might be. We think ahead to that day when we shall lie there. What sort of record will we have accumulated to bring into the presence of the Almighty? This process of looking seriously at ourselves, in the light of eternity, may not be a pleasant one, but it is very necessary if we are to live the lives we ought to live. As we stand before the casket of one of God's great saints who has passed to his reward, we are conscious that his life reflects a judgment upon ours that we cannot escape. His accomplishments challenge us to spend the rest of our days in service that will really count for something in the sight of God. When we receive such insight, the day of death is better for us than the day of birth.

The time of death is also a time of leaving an old environment, and a time of introduction into a new kind of life. When a child is born, we know only too well the kind of world into which he is introduced. Our existence is one of pain and suffering of the body and of the mind. We know that the only true happiness in this life lies in following the will of God, but we are surrounded with temptations calling upon us to ignore God, live for ourselves, and thus destroy ourselves. We think of the endless conflicts of this world— the members of a family set one against the other, the bitterness and argument that can arise in a neighborhood, the wars as nation sets upon nation and the lives of thousands

37

are destroyed in a few seconds of time. We think of the process of aging which we all experience throughout life. Our senses are taken from us, one by one, the eyes growing blind and the ears deaf. Of course, life has its compensations for all these things, but we cannot help but wonder about our feelings when a child is born into the world. If we were less selfish and more concerned for the feelings of the child, perhaps we would make the day of birth a day of mourning over all the trials that lie ahead of the new babe.

How different is that transition when one leaves this world! Then we move into the Father's house. Sorrows and tears are things of the past. Fellowship with loved ones is renewed and even strengthened in the perfect communication that overcomes all misunderstandings. We live together in the light of the love of God, in the blessing of his presence. We can join in that shout which was heard by the author of the last book in our New Testament, "Blessed are the dead who die in the Lord" (Rev. 14:13). Thus our faith leads us to the understanding: the day of death is better than the day of birth. It is our graduation day, when we leave the earth behind and go to be with our Lord.

Our Father, give us of thine own understanding as we face the sorrows of parting. We know that thou hast guided us through our sojourn here. Give us the faith to trust our loved ones to thee, in that eternal life which thou hast prepared for us all, as together we anticipate the joyous reunion when we shall all be together again in thy house; through Jesus Christ our Lord. Amen.

7

God's View of Death

Psalms 116:15

Our feelings in the face of death may be difficult to describe, but they are common to all mankind. We term the loss of a loved one sad, tragic, unfortunate, sorrowful, or painful. In spite of the fact that we know death eventually comes to all of us, we fight against it with all our strength and with all the knowledge that science can provide. Thus, when we turn to the book of the Psalms and read that the death of a saint is "precious" in the sight of the Lord, the statement seems too difficult for us to grasp.

We hold many things precious, but death is not one of them. For us, life is precious, friends are precious, our possessions are precious. But at death we leave our possessions behind, say farewell to our friends, and depart from life. How can death be called "precious" in anyone's sight?

The scripture does not say that all death is regarded as precious. For the Christian, death is still an enemy which must be endured for a time until God sets all things aright. Then, eventually, death will be destroyed. Until that time, the end of this life is a time of sorrow and pain and parting. But in some cases, death takes on a new meaning. For these few, death is precious, even though it may be tragic for the rest of mankind. Precious, in the sight of God, is the death of his saints.

For a few moments, let us try to see with the eyes of God, to understand with a divine understanding. We gather to pay tribute to one of these saints who has departed from us. This event, so sorrowful for us, is precious in the sight of the Lord. Perhaps he will give us the grace to see our loss in the same way that he views it. Something about the death of a saint makes it an event of unequaled value in his sight.

The first answer would seem to lie in the nature of the saint. Death is precious because a saint has died. And the Bible tells us a curious thing about saints: they die long before they come to the end of this life. Jesus taught that if we are going to come after him, we must deny ourselves and take up a cross and follow him. His hearers understood what he meant, for they knew that a cross was the instrument of death. Each new follower of Christ portrays his obedience to this command in the act of Christian baptism. This act, symbolic of the process of becoming a Christian, represents the death, burial, and resurrection of the individual. The true Christian, then, the one who has become a saint, has already died, been buried, and has been raised or reborn in the image of Christ. When he comes to the end of this physical existence, he does not really experience death at all. He possesses a divine life which he has received from God. These physical changes that cause us such sorrow are not really death for the saint but merely a process of change, of translation, of growth into a new sphere of living. How precious is this step in the life of the saint!

The death of the saint is also precious because of what he

leaves behind. We may cling to this life, but we recognize that it is an imperfect thing at best. In many respects the true saint has a more difficult time than the rest. Our world is so bent and twisted by sin. The daily paper is a record of lives gone wrong, of God denied, of man destroying himself. Most of us get used to these things, but the true saint never does. He shares God's sorrow at the sin and yearns with the very love of God toward the sinner. Most of us can ignore suffering and injustice, but the saint cannot. He may spend his entire life in trying to remedy some little thing that the rest of us feel cannot be changed anyway. We admire our saints and recognize that they have been responsible for so many of the finer things in life that we enjoy, but few of us would change places with them. Eventually, however, the time comes when the saint is released from his labor and goes to his Master to receive that "Well done, thou good and faithful servant." Precious in the Lord's sight is the death of his saints, and great the rejoicing that their mission is accomplished.

The saint leaves his trials and labors behind at death, but he also has a right to look forward to that which comes afterward. He leaves this life in order to go home. Thus his death must be particularly precious to his Heavenly Father.

God loves all of us, saint and sinner alike, with a love that we can only begin to understand. We are his children, created in his image. The love that we hold for our own children indicates, in a small and limited way, the love that God has for us. Our love, even at best, is touched with selfishness and limited by our lack of understanding. God's love is pure and holy; it proceeds from a heart that knows us even better than we know ourselves. His love is so great

41

that the Bible tells us he gave his only Son as a sacrifice for us that the broken fellowship between ourselves and God might be restored. God is like that father in the story Jesus told, who would not stop his son from moving to a far country and wasting all his possessions foolishly, but who received the prodigal with joyous celebration upon his return. God has done everything he could to restore us to himself. Even while we were sinners, Christ died for us. (Rom. 5:8.)

We sometimes think of a saint as a particularly holy person, but this idea is only partly true. No human being is really righteous in the sight of the Holy God. The saint is just an ordinary person who has turned from his own selfish way in order to accept God's sacrifice for him. He has no righteousness of his own, but through faith he partakes of the righteousness of Christ and is born again into the family of God. Thus the prodigal comes home, the lost sheep is found, God's yearning love is satisfied, and the saint gets to be a saint. Even the angels in heaven rejoice, we are told, when a sinner is transformed in this way. (Luke 15:10.)

Yet the new saint still lives in this dwelling place of flesh. He still struggles with sorrow and temptation, with doubts and uncertainties. He tries to do the will of his Father, but often he does not understand the Father's will or he is too weak to carry it out. Then, one day the call comes for him to return home. What joy must fill our Heavenly Father's heart as he comes. At last the family circle is complete. Barriers to understanding are wiped away. God can express his love to his children in all its richness and its fullness. Precious in the sight of the Lord is the death of his saints.

As we gather in our sorrow, let us seek some measure of understanding of the mind of God. The one we love has been translated into a new life. He has left behind the sorrows of this world and moved into his Father's house. The valley of the shadow is past; he dwells now in the presence of the Lord forever.

Our Father, our sorrow overcomes us at the sense of the loss that is ours. Still, even in this hour, we ask that thou wouldst share with us a measure of thy joy. We give thanks for the example in living that these saints set for us. Help us to be worthy of such examples until thy call comes to us also. We ask in the name of Christ, our Lord. Amen.

8

The Mystery of Death

I Corinthians 15:51

We live in a mysterious world, surrounded with things we do not understand. We touch a switch on the wall, and the room is flooded with light. Yet not one of us can really explain how that light came to be. We turn on our television sets, and from the void around us come pictures with voices and music. How can scenes and events taking place thousands of miles away appear at almost the same instant in our living rooms? Not even the wisest of us can give a complete and accurate answer.

Most men do not trouble themselves with trying to explain these things. We are content if our rooms are lighted and if our television brings us entertainment. We do not need to understand how these strange forces operate in order to utilize them for our benefit.

None of these mysteries of our world is quite as dark as the mystery of which the apostle speaks in his letter to the Corinthian church. Nothing puzzles us more than the things pertaining to life after death. Then the apostle tells us that we shall not all sleep, but at the end we shall all be changed. As we gather in memory of a loved one who has been taken from us, sorrowing in the face of death, nothing is more difficult for us to grasp than the great hope of the resurrection. Yet, in this hour, the understanding of these things seems more important than anything else in all the world.

The apostle, however, does not explain the transformation that he predicts; he merely states the fact. Our curiosity and our need are left unsatisfied. In the two thousand years that have passed since he wrote, no one else has been able to clarify the resurrection any more than he did. If we must wait until the mystery has been dispelled before we can believe in the resurrection, we may wait forever. On the other hand, we can treat this matter as we do all the other things in nature that we cannot understand. We can accept it by faith and let it bring meaning to those aspects of life that concern us the most.

One problem which concerns all of us is the nature of life itself. The scientist can tell us many things about it. Our knowledge can improve it and make it easier. But the true nature of our life here is still a mystery.

If we turn to the Bible for an answer, we can also learn many things about life. It is described as a shadow (Job 8:9) or as a breath (Job 7:7). It is like a tent, easily plucked up and moved as a wandering shepherd moves. (Isa. 38:12.) It moves as quickly as a weaver's shuttle. (Job 7:6.) Life is a flower that blooms but immediately fades, like the grass that grows and begins to wither. (Isa. 40:6-7.) All these things speak of the brevity of life; not one explains its true nature.

When we view life in terms of the resurrection, however, we gain a new understanding. Life is something more than our brief span here on earth. Back in the beginning, when

God first brought man into being, the Bible says that he breathed into man the breath of life, and man became a living soul. Something within man partakes of the very life of God. Man may live in the world, but he possesses something of eternity. Thus he can look forward to the time when he shall be changed, in a moment, in the twinkling of an eye. The resurrection may be a mystery, but it reveals to us something of the true nature of life.

The other great problem that we face in times such as these is the problem of death. What is this experience, this ending, which all of us must face? The scientist can explain some of the diseases which overcome us or describe the changes in our physical bodies, but death itself is still a mystery to man.

Only when we view death in terms of our faith in the resurrection does it take on its true meaning. Then we understand what the psalmist means in talking about the valley of the shadow of death, with the home of the Lord beyond it in which the table is spread for us. (Ps. 23:4-5.) We can understand what the apostle means when he says, "We shall not all sleep." Death is a sleep, leading to a waking in the glorious dawn. This is the reason that Jesus spoke of his friend Lazarus as having fallen asleep in death. (John 11:11.) Paul wrote of death as an enemy, destroyed in the great victory of the resurrection. (I Cor. 15:26.) Jesus thought of death as the way home, the way back to the Father's house, in which rooms are prepared for all of us. (John 14:2.)

What is death? Seen in terms of the resurrection, it is no more than a passing incident in the great pattern of life. It marks the end of our short visit here, and our return to

46

our true home. Just as Mother and Dad are overjoyed when the children return from their travels, so must the heart of God be filled with joy as his children come back to the Father's house.

> It seemeth such a little way to me,
> Across to that strange country, the Beyond;
> And yet, not strange, for it has grown to be
> The home of those of whom I am so fond;
> They make it seem familiar and most dear,
> As journeying friends bring distant countries near.
>
> And so for me there is no sting to death,
> And so the grave has lost its victory;
> It is but crossing with abated breath
> And white, set face, a little strip of sea,
> To find the loved ones waiting on the shore,
> More beautiful, more precious than before.[1]

Heavenly Father, we confess that we cannot understand the mystery of the resurrection. Yet we ask that thou wouldst fill our hearts with the certainty of its hope, that we may better understand the nature of life and this change that we call death. We ask in the name of the Christ, who rose as the firstfruits of all who sleep. Amen.

[1] Ella Wheeler Wilcox, "The Beyond." Reprinted by permission of Rand McNally & Company.

9

The Universal Question

Job 14:14
"If a man die, shall he live again?" Poor, broken Job raised the question in the agony of his loss and suffering. But his question is also ours, for each of us eventually raises it. Is there anything beyond the grave? If a man die, shall he live again?

We're interested in the answer for two reasons, or in two situations. First, we stand at the grave of a loved one and say a last farewell. Then the question faces us. Is this, indeed, the last? Is there no hope that we shall see again those who have departed from us? And then, we raise the question in the face of our own fears. Each of us knows that life must end in the experience we call death. Will this be the end for us? When we die, shall we live again?

Our questions are not left unanswered, and our listening hope and love do hear the flutter of a wing. Our ears catch the voice of intuition, and it softly tells us that the grave cannot be the end. Our world is so badly out of joint, with right forever on the cross and wrong forever on the throne. So much that is evil seems to triumph, and so much that is good to die in bitter disappointment. A man may reach the

48

peak of his creative powers, just ready to make some great contribution to mankind, when death strikes him low and all his abilities are taken out of the world. We cannot believe that life is really like this. There must be more goodness, more sense to existence than we can see from our viewpoint within time and space. Beyond the grave must lie a new kind of life where everything is straightened out and put right, and where that which seems to be wasted here is put to use.

Strangely enough, man always seems to be able to sense this life beyond. Go where you will among the races of mankind, and you will find belief in immortality. Do not limit yourselves to Christian lands. Find those who never heard of Christ, who have never read a Bible. Look at those with no consciousness of a Heavenly Father, those who may worship a stream or a rock or a tree, those who see life as a constant struggle with evil demons. Even these will look upon the grave with hope, will bury the bones of their dead in anticipation of a resurrection, or will bring gifts of food for the spirit to enjoy in the other world. If a man die, shall he live again? The voice of intuition responds, "Yes."

If we turn to nature itself, the answer also seems to be certain. Jesus spoke about the grain of wheat which must fall into the earth and die or it would abide by itself alone. If it dies, however, it bears much fruit. We see the life of man pictured in the cycle of the seasons. The autumn must follow the summer; the leaves turn brown, and the trees apparently die. Then comes the winter, and the cold, dead landscape is covered with a blanket of white. Still, beneath the soil life remains. With the warmth of the spring, the seeds stir and put forth their shoots. Soon green fingers reach through the black soil, and buds appear on the trees. Flowers burst into bloom, and all nature sings the song of life renewed. If a man die, shall he live again? The voice of nature responds, "Yes."

The Christian, however, looks beyond all these things for the answer to his question. For him, God's revelation of himself is far more meaningful than anything found within man or within nature. Turn, then, to the Bible and raise the question: if a man die, shall he live again?

Even Job in his hopelessness did not feel that all was lost. "I know that my Redeemer lives," he told his friends. (Job 19:25.) And David, grief-stricken at the side of his little dead son, was able to put away his grief. "I know I can do nothing to bring him back," he said, "but some day I expect to go to be with him." (II Sam. 12:23.) The valley of the shadow of death seems to hold no fears for those who have some understanding of the love of an almighty God. (Ps. 23:4.)

God's revelation of himself is completed in the person of our Lord. Thus our Bibles, following the resurrection of Christ, ring with the triumphant affirmative answer to our question. We ask the apostle Paul, "Shall a man live again?" As he looks at these mortal bodies of ours, he replies, "I know that if this earthly body in which I dwell should be dissolved, I shall have a body from God, a dwelling place not made by hands, eternal, in heaven" (II Cor. 5:1). We turn to John, the writer of those beautiful New Testament letters, and ask him, "Shall a man live again?" He responds, "I know that I'm a child of God. I don't know what I may look like in the future, but I know that when the Lord appears, I'm going to be just like him. I'm going to see him as he is" (I John 3:2).

Finally, we turn to our Lord himself. "Shall a man live again?" He turns to us with the quiet smile of assurance and authority. "I am the resurrection and the life. Whoever believes in me, even though he dies, yet he shall live, and whoever lives and believes in me shall never die." (John 11:25.)

The grave is not an end but a beginning. Even in our sorrow, the answer of faith rings clear. If a man die, shall he live again? The voices of intuition, nature, and revelation join in the reply: As he lives, so we shall live also.

> No, not cold beneath the grasses,
>   Not close-walled within the tomb;
> Rather, in our Father's Mansion,
>   Living in another room.
>
> Living, like the one who loves me,
>   Like yon child with cheeks abloom,
> Out of sight, at desk or schoolbook,
>   Busy in another room.
>
> Nearer than the youth whom fortune
>   Beckons where the strange lands loom;
> Just behind the hanging curtain,
>   Serving in another room.
>
> Shall I doubt my Father's mercy?
>   Shall I think of death as doom,
> Or the stepping o'er the threshold
>   To a bigger, brighter room?
>
> Shall I blame my Father's wisdom?
>   Shall I sit enswathed in gloom,

When I know my Love is happy,
Waiting in another room? [1]

Lord of all life, open our ears to hear. Strengthen our faith that as thou didst bring our Lord Jesus again from the dead, so we shall know the joys of life everlasting, as we pray in his name. Amen.

[1] Robert Freeman, "In My Father's House." Reprinted by permission of Robert G. Freeman.

10

For a Faithful Servant

Matthew 25:23
Jesus taught that the measure of true greatness is to be found in service. When we come to the end of life and look back upon how we have spent our days, the important thing is not the power we have gained, the reputation we have achieved, or the property we have accumulated. The thing that matters is the service we have rendered. Our Lord came not to be ministered unto, but to minister and to give his life. (Matt. 20:28.) He demanded the ultimate loyalty of his followers, and yet he was willing to take the place of the humblest servant, stoop, and wash the feet of his disciples. (John 13:5.) Just as he predicted, those who are really greatest among us are those who have served the most. (Matt. 20:26.)

Jesus' parable of the talents has much to teach us about the nature of this service which is the duty and the glory of his followers in this life. First, we notice that God gives each of us the means by which we are to serve. Each man in the story was entrusted with a talent according to his ability. Each man can use only that which he receives. Everyone receives something, and God holds everyone responsible for the use of what he gets. We should not envy those who seem to enjoy all the blessings of life, for they have greater responsibilities. The true saint is one who takes what he is given and uses it in service in the name of his Lord.

Next, we notice in the parable that God expects loyal service from all his children. The first two men in the story were entrusted with different amounts. However, each man was faithful to his stewardship and doubled the amount given him, and each man received exactly the same praise from his Lord. God does not seem to be concerned about the size of the talent he has given us in life, or about the grandeur of the service that we are able to offer him. He cares about the faithfulness of our service. He values the little things that are done lovingly and consistently in his name. Even a cool glass of water given to the thirsty, food for the hungry, clothing for the naked, or a visit to the lonely offered from a sympathetic and compassionate heart are counted as services rendered to the Christ himself. (Matt. 25:35-40.)

We remember the time when Jesus stood beside the treasury of the temple of his day and watched the people bringing their offerings. (Mark 12:41-44.) He saw the poor widow putting in her pennies, and he told his disciples that she had given more than all the rest. The important fact was not the total amount she had given, but that she had given everything she had. When the heart is right and one's dedication is complete, God's response is always the same: "Well done, good and faithful servant." It's not the size of the gift that matters, but the size of the heart of the giver.

We gather today in memory of one we have loved who

has been taken from us. At such a time, wealth and reputation, power and intellect are no longer of great importance. It is the lifetime of service that we honor, time spent in giving rather than getting. In these moments, we echo the words of our Lord, "Well done, good and faithful servant."

The parable does not stop here but speaks also of the rewards of service. Each faithful steward was told to enter into the joy of his Lord. Our service here on earth seems to be but an apprenticeship to a greater service which someday we will be privileged to perform.

What is this joy that is to be the reward of the Lord's obedient servants? It certainly includes the joy of salvation, and the eternal life which we begin to experience here before our days on earth are ended. When the Bible describes the conversion of an individual, his acceptance of Christ as Savior, that account frequently takes notice of the joy experienced. A jailor in the city of Philippi was about to commit suicide when he heard the preaching of the apostle Paul. He was obedient to the gospel that he heard that night, and the account that we have leaves him rejoicing with all that were in his house. (Acts 16:25-34.) Or we read the story of the evangelist who was given the opportunity to witness to an official of the Ethiopian court. This officer also heard the message and was obedient to it, and he went on his way rejoicing. (Acts 8:26-39.) The primary Christian experience is one of joy.

This joy is also the characteristic experience of the Christian life. The apostle Paul, in spite of the problems and persecutions that he had to face, commanded his followers, "Rejoice in the Lord always" (Phil. 4:4). On one occasion when he stood in court to defend himself, he began with the words, "I count myself happy" (Acts 26:2). Jesus began his great Sermon on the Mount, perhaps the basic document of all Christian ethics, with the words, "Happy are the poor in spirit, for theirs is the kingdom of Heaven (Matt. 5:3). Why shouldn't the Christian be happy? His is the joy of service. His is the joy of friendship and fellowship. His is the life of love and of hope. He has every right to be happy, for he is a son of God.

The hope of the Christian life extends beyond this physical existence to the joy of the eternal life which has been prepared for us. The scripture says of Jesus that he endured the suffering and humiliation of the cross for the sake of the joy that was set before him, the joy of the reunion with his Father. (Heb. 12:2.) John, the author of the last book in our New Testament, was commanded to write that "happy are the dead who die in the Lord." They experience the joy of rest from their labors, and their works will follow after them. (Rev. 14:13.) Nothing that they have done will be wasted, but their efforts will ultimately receive a reward. The apostle Paul looked beyond the close of his earthly life and spoke of the crown of righteousness that was laid up for him, a reward which the Lord would give him in that final day. (II Tim. 4:8.) These hopes are not idle dreams but promises of God to those who are faithful in service to him.

In these moments of sadness, as we gather in memory of a faithful saint who has departed from us, let us hear the words of the Master as he welcomes him home: "Well done, good and faithful servant. Enter into the joy of your Lord."

I cannot say, and I will not say
That he is dead. He is just away.

With a cheery smile, and a wave of the hand,
He has wandered into an unknown land.

And left us dreaming how very fair
It needs must be since he lingers there.

And you—O you, who the wildest yearn
For the old-time step and the glad return—

Think of him faring on, as dear
In the love of there as the love of here;

Think of him still as the same, I say;
He is not dead—he is just away.[1]

Our Father, the only source of true joy, we thank thee for the privileges of service. May the lives of these good and faithful ones inspire us to more devoted obedience to thy commands. Help us to experience the joy that overcomes all sorrow, even the joy that comes from the assurance of thy love; through Christ our Lord. Amen.

[1] James Whitcomb Riley, "Away."

11

The Man of Faith

Acts 11:24

Can a life be summarized in a few words? Even when we meet in memory of the beloved dead, we hesitate to try. All the complex values and motives, the depths of the human emotions, the heights of intellectual achievement cannot hope to be comprehended in some short, simple statement. And yet, sometimes the truly great have a divine simplicity about them which may be briefly pointed out, and then nothing further need be added. Such is the case with this man Barnabas, a man who could be described as a good person, full of faith and of the Spirit of God. Some of the saints in our own day are like him. Any praises that we might heap upon them are superfluous; we only thank God that we have been given the privilege of having them with us for a time.

Notice the qualities that marked this Barnabas as a saint. He was a good man. Evidently he was a man of some property. The Bible tells us that he sold a field and brought the entire proceeds of the sale to the leaders of his church to be used to help the poor. (Acts 4:37.) The whole church apparently trusted his judgment. When Saul of Tarsus claimed to have become a Christian, and the whole church wondered whether to trust him or not, Barnabas stood up for him and won the church over to give him a chance. (Acts 9:26-27.) Barnabas was good-hearted, trustworthy, and even those who knew him best recognized these qualities. We thank God for those we have known in our own day who have proved equally sensitive to human need and equally willing to be friends to the friendless. These are good men.

Even the best of us is not perfect, and our goodness is always spoiled to some degree by our mistakes and flaws. Life demands something more than sheer goodness from us, and Barnabas had more to offer. The scripture says that he was a man of faith and that the very spirit of God was within him. These words do not refer to some blessing that he received because he was unusually good. On the contrary, they mean that his goodness was an outgrowth of a divine power possessing him and making him the saint that he was. He was a man of faith.

We know something of his faith in Jesus Christ, for we find him active in the early church at a time when such activity could mean imprisonment or even death. We can imagine Barnabas at that point in life when his faith first demanded some act of decision or identification with those early Christians. Would he have the courage to commit his life to Jesus Christ, to unite with his persecuted band of followers, to give up friends and possessions for a new way of life? We cannot know the depths of the struggle that Barnabas experienced, but we do know its outcome. He was a man of faith in Christ who had accepted Jesus as Lord.

Barnabas also had faith in men, a fact that he demonstrated when he so readily accepted Saul of Tarsus. The act seems simple to us, for we know that the young man was destined to become the apostle Paul, the writer of a good portion of our New Testament and the great missionary to the Gentiles. But Barnabas could not have suspected these things. He only knew Saul as an outcast, rejected by Jews because of his new faith in Jesus and by Christians because of his old acts of persecution of the church. No one but Barnabas would have faith in him.

In later years, Paul, Barnabas, and a young man named John Mark were called upon to make a missionary trip for their church. (Acts 13:1-5.) Mark was an eager participant until they reached a part of Asia Minor where travel was both difficult and dangerous. Then Mark deserted his friends and ran home to safety. (Acts 13:13.) His conduct was too much for Paul, who refused to take him along on the next trip. But Barnabas could have faith even in a deserter. He was willing to accept Mark as a companion in his subsequent travels (Acts 15:39), and he became instrumental in restoring the friendship between Mark and Paul. (II Tim. 4:11.) Barnabas had faith in men.

He also had faith in the church. He knew its weaknesses and shortcomings. He knew of sin within the church. (Acts 5:1-11.) He watched arguments and disagreements develop. (Acts 15:1-12.) But in all these things he remained not only faithful but active. He gave himself fully to Christ's service. He was willing to risk his life in missionary work. In all, he was a man of faith filled with the Holy Spirit.

The Bible tells us the results of these qualities. Because of the kind of man Barnabas was, many were added to the Lord. We know from experience that this is not an isolated story of one man two thousand years ago. These results have been repeated over and over in the history of Christianity as good men and women, filled with faith and with the Spirit of God, have lived and died in such a way that others could come to know Christ. Most of us would freely confess that our own salvation has come from dedicated men and women like Barnabas.

So we gather this day in triumphant tribute to the saints whom God has given to live among us. We think not just of one who has departed, but of all those good men and women, filled with faith and the Spirit of God, who have gone before us. Each one goes to his individual reward, but each leaves a heritage here whose limit cannot be measured.

In Yosemite National Park in California, a large granite boulder has been transformed into a memorial by a bronze plaque which has been attached to the rock. A man's profile is outlined in relief on that plaque. Beneath the picture are these words: "Stephen Ting Mather. Born July 4, 1867. Died January 22, 1930. He laid the foundation of the National Park Service, defining and establishing the policies under which its areas shall be developed and conserved unimpaired for future generations. There will never come an end to the good he has done."

As the poet has said,

> Lives of great men all remind us
>   We can make our lives sublime,
> And, departing, leave behind us
>   Footprints on the sands of time.

61

> Footprints, that perhaps another,
>   Sailing o'er life's solemn main,
> A forlorn and shipwrecked brother,
>   Seeing, shall take heart again.
>
> Let us then be up and doing,
>   With a heart for any fate;
> Still achieving, still pursuing,
>   Learn to labor and to wait.[1]

Our Father, give us a true appreciation of these saints who have gone before us. We know that because they lived in thee, there will never come an end to the good they have done. Give us grace that our lives may be more worthy of the example they have set for us; through Jesus Christ our Lord. Amen.

---

[1] Henry Wadsworth Longfellow, "The Psalm of Life."

12

A Glad Reunion

Revelation 21:1

John was in exile on the island of Patmos, an old man, tired and alone. The other apostles had long since been martyred for their faith. John knew that the end could not be far off for him. It was Sunday, the Lord's Day, the day of worship. Miles away, his Christian friends were assembling for the church service. Wishing that he might be with them, John knelt in silent prayer.

Then the vision came to him. He heard a voice, strange but yet familiar, a voice that he had listened to so eagerly many years before. Now it rang in his ears like a trumpet's blast. Turning about, John saw a familiar face, features he had not seen for a long time but that he could never forget. He recognized the face, but it looked so different. John remembered one night that he had spent on top of a high mountain. The Lord had looked much the same way then. (Luke 9:29.) John knew it was the Christ, and he fell on his face to worship.

Jesus Christ had many things to reveal to John on that Sunday. There were messages to be sent to some of the churches. There were predictions of things about to take place. John was given a vision of the Holy City, the new Jerusalem. He was given a word of hope to be spoken to all Christians in those difficult days of persecution and death. Sometime everything would be set right. There would be a new heaven and a new earth. Mourning and crying and pain would all be ended. Death would be no more. All things would be made new. One strange fact impressed John so much that he made special mention of it in his description of this new existence to come: the sea would be no more.

We wonder at this unusual item in the list. If there is to be a new earth, many things now familiar to us will be abolished. We can understand why tears should be wiped away, for these are symbolic of our sorrow. We can understand why pain and death should end, and we long for the day when this promise will be fulfilled. But why does John call our attention to the absence of the sea? Perhaps he intended to remind us of some of the great aspects of our Christian hope.

For one thing, the sea speaks to us of unrest. Its waves are never still. The day may be calm, but the tides still move up and down, the billows still shatter themselves against the rocks. Let the wind blow and the storm lash the waters, and even our strongest ships are in danger. Perhaps we like to watch the waves because they remind us so much of our own lives. We too are always in turmoil and never at rest. Nothing seems to remain the same; everything constantly changes. We remember happy days that we wish we could bring back, but they are gone forever. We seem to be always striving, always running, always on the move but never quite sure of where we are going.

Even when our bodies rest, our minds are not at peace. We long for some escape, an opportunity to stop and see where we are, to recover our strength, to find peace. In our weariness we hear the promise: the sea shall be no more. We go to that place which our Lord has prepared for us, and there at last we shall find peace and rest.

To the apostle, and to us as well, the sea spoke of mystery. It marked a fearful boundary for the ancient, who thought of sailing to the edge of the earth and then dropping off. Most navigators were content to stay near the shore, creeping from port to port. The sea contained fearful monsters and unknown terrors that the human mind could not even imagine. Every captain had his tales of lost companions, of ships that had put bravely forth, never to return. In our day, some of the mystery has gone, but not all. We have mapped the borders of the oceans and explored some of their depths, but much more remains to be learned.

Just as the ancient world was bounded by the sea, so our lives are surrounded by mystery. We know not whence we came into this existence, and we know not whither we go. The true nature of life itself is a mystery still, and all our sciences have brought us no word about life after death. In the time of sorrow it seems to us that the knowledge we most need is the knowledge we do not have. The things we most desire to know remain a mystery. But someday the sea will be no more. We will understand all things then; life and death, the purpose of it all, and the destiny that our loving Father has in mind for us. Until that day we walk in faith, but nevertheless, we long for the time to come when these mysteries will be explained.

The sea also speaks of separation. On that ancient Sunday it kept John from his friends. It was the mark of his exile, the jailor that imprisoned him on his island. We can imagine him looking across the waves toward the distant horizon, catching in his mind the towering buildings of the city of Ephesus. There was his home. He thought of his church and of the friends he had known and loved over the years. How he must have wished that, like Moses, he could stretch out a rod and part the waves and walk on the dry land to visit his comrades. But he could not, and day followed empty day in loneliness. We have the same experience as we watch our friends wave good-bye to us as they leave on some ocean voyage. We would not keep them back with us, and we are not able to go with them. We wish them well, but we think sadly of the miles of water that separate us.

The experience of death is the great separation. Our faith tells us that a good God would not allow this experience to be ultimately evil. We hesitate to pray that our loved one should endure further pain and suffering here, and yet our love cannot give him up. Our sorrow is for the loss, the separation. We think of the days and weeks that must pass with no sight of the departed, with no word exchanged between us.

Again we hear the promise: the sea will be no more. The time of separation will be ended. We shall all be together once again, in the Father's kingdom. This promise renews our hope until that day when we too depart to join those we have loved on the farther shore.

Sunset and evening star,
And one clear call for me!

And may there be no moaning of the bar,
　When I put out to sea,

But such a tide as moving seems asleep,
　Too full for sound and foam,
When that which drew from out the boundless deep
　Turns again home.

Twilight and evening bell,
　And after that the dark!
And may there be no sadness of farewell,
　When I embark;

For tho' from out our bourne of Time and Place
　The flood may bear me far,
I hope to see my Pilot face to face
　When I have crost the bar.[1]

Our Father, we give thanks for the wonderful promises of thy word. We long for the day when we shall finally be at peace, when all mysteries will be made plain, and when the long days of separation will end. Comfort us with this living hope; through Jesus Christ our Lord. Amen.

[1] Alfred Lord Tennyson, "Crossing the Bar."

13

Some Thoughts on Suicide

Romans 8:38-39; Galatians 6:2-5

There is a natural time for all to die. Man is not an immortal, but a creature of time and of place. None of us lives forever. Each of us, in the wisdom of God, has an allotted span of life, and we cannot go beyond it. Death is as much a part of our experience here on earth as birth or growth or aging. Sometimes, however, a life is cut short, its days unfulfilled. We are shocked and saddened at the loss, and we wonder at the terrible burdens, the unknown pains of body or spirit, which could lead to such an event.

All of us have learned that we have burdens to bear. Sometimes these are burdens of the flesh—the physical agony, the loss of a limb, the deterioration of one of our bodily faculties. Other suffering is not of the body at all but of the mind. Perhaps these burdens are the heaviest, for they affect all our relationships and even warp our understanding. Mental suffering is invisible, and the loving help of friends and relatives is often unavailable to us because they have no idea that the burden even exists.

Such burdens may become so heavy that at times they seem almost impossible for us to bear. Like King David of old, we are overwhelmed. We cry out, "O that I had the wings of a dove. I would fly away to the wilderness, and there at last I would find rest" (Ps. 55:6-7). Such feeling is not strange or unusual, but a feeling we have all experienced as our problems seem to grow too great for our strength.

Once in awhile we know someone, like the one in whose memory we gather today, who succumbs to his burdens. Perhaps the problems he faced, which we can never really know, were beyond the strength of any human being. Perhaps his strength, sapped by the passing of time and weakened by the constant struggle, was simply not equal to its task. Perhaps the fault was really ours. The Scriptures command us to bear one another's burdens. (Gal. 6:2.) If we could only know the troubles of others, we might help them carry the load and thus make life more enjoyable for them. But sometimes we are insensitive to their needs, and at other times no one could possibly know what the real burdens are.

Is there any hope as we face this tragedy of our human condition, this darkness that enfolds not only this one life but also the very essence of our human experience itself? Yes, our faith in God can sustain us even in this hour. In fact, this faith is the only comfort available to us.

The very basis of the Christian gospel is the love of God which extends to every individual. There are no exceptions; God loves us all. No one can rise too high, and no one has ever fallen too low, to be beyond the reach of his love in Christ Jesus. The Scriptures remind us that nothing in all creation, not even the fact of death itself, can separate us from that love. (Rom. 8:38-39.) We know that our sin

69

does not stop God from loving us. In fact, as we remember the ministry of our Lord, the depths of sin seem to call forth additional resources of love in return. (Rom. 5:20.) The ministry of Christ was predominantly to the sick, the outcast, the sinful, and the discouraged. (Luke 4:21.) They were in need of a Savior, and he came to heal and forgive and save those who were lost. (Luke 19:10.) If Jesus taught us anything about God at all, he taught us that God is love (I John 4:8), and that he cares for us just as any father cares for his children.

Think what this fact means, that God cares for us. His love is not an idle emotion, a feeling of sympathy as he watches us struggle with burdens too great for our strength. God takes care of us just as he takes care of every other part of this universe of his. Not a sparrow falls to the ground but that he knows about it. (Matt. 10:29.) The very hairs of our heads are numbered. (Matt. 10:30.) God takes note of the slightest incident, of things that we would scarcely notice, and he incorporates them all into his great plan for this whole universe. (Rom. 8:28.) How much more, then, does he care about these tragic events that bring us together in sorrow this day!

The One who so loves and cares is the only One who can really understand the things we do. Our acts remain a mystery to those around us, even to those who love us best. Much of what we do remains a mystery to us, for we either do not know or will not face the causes of our actions. We deceive ourselves and others by the reasons that we invent, and other people often make matters worse by attributing the things we do to the worst possible motives. But God understands everything about us. He is not misled by the criticisms of others. He is not deceived by our own feelings about ourselves. He looks deep into each heart and understands the true causes and the real motives. Upon the depths of his understanding, the extent of his care, and the power of his love we may rest our faith.

So much about ourselves and about those we love must always be mysterious to us. Many things are concealed, and our finite minds would not be able to grasp the divine pattern even if all the facts were known. We must trust in the love and understanding of the all-wise God in the assurance that someday all things will be made plain.

> Not now, but in the coming years,
> It may be in the better land,
> We'll read the meaning of our tears,
> And there, sometime, we'll understand.
>
> We'll catch the broken threads again,
> And finish what we here began;
> Heaven will the mysteries explain,
> And then, ah, then, we'll understand.
>
> We'll know why clouds instead of sun
> Were over many a cherished plan;
> Why song has ceased when scarce begun;
> 'Tis there, sometime, we'll understand.
>
> God knows the way, He holds the key,
> He guides us with unerring hand;
> Sometime with tearless eyes we'll see;
> Yes, there, up there, we'll understand.
>
> Then trust in God through all thy days;
> Fear not! for He doth hold thy hand;

Though dark thy way, still sing and praise:
Some time, some time, we'll understand.[1]

*Father of all mercies, teach us to trust thee when trust
seems the most difficult. We rely on thy wisdom and thy
love. Let these be sufficient to give us comfort now and hope
for the future; through Jesus Christ our Lord. Amen.*

[1] Maxwell N. Cornelius, "Some Time We'll Understand."

14

On the Loss of a Little Child

II Samuel 12:23

Death takes all of our dear ones eventually, for each of us must die. We are not surprised when our grandparents die, for they have lived rich, full lives and their time has come. Our parents also depart, and while our sense of loss is more acute, the parting is simply one of those events which must be accepted as a part of life. But when our children are taken, the tragedy overwhelms us, and we cry out, in rebellion, that such things should not happen. Yet we know, of course, that they do happen.

Just such rebellion was in the heart of King David of Israel long ago. His little son had been taken seriously ill. For a week he lingered between life and death. David did everything possible to save him. The best physicians of the day were consulted, we may be sure. David also turned to God in prayer. He fasted and spent entire nights prostrate upon the ground in supplication. The members of his court urged him to get up or to eat something, but he would not. His son was ill, and perhaps his prayers could have some effect in bringing about the recovery of the boy.

All these things were of no avail. At the end of the week

73

the child died. The agony of the father had been so extreme during the illness that the servants were afraid to tell him that the child was dead. "If he acts like that when the boy is only ill," they said, "what will he do when he learns that the child is gone? He may even harm himself." But the secret could not be kept, and the king had to be told the child was dead.

Then, to the amazement of all who watched, David arose from the ground, washed, put on his robes, and went to the House of God to worship the Almighty. When he returned to the palace, he asked the servants for food. They prepared the meal, and he sat down and ate. The others couldn't understand such behavior. "How is this?" they asked. "When the child was merely ill, you fasted and wept for him and carried on as though the affliction were more than you could bear. But now that the child is actually dead, you give up your mourning and weeping entirely."

David's answer was simple and obvious. "I wept and prayed in the hope that God would let the child live. Now that I know the child is gone, why should I continue to fast and weep? I know that nothing I can do will bring him back again."

David's behavior seems so strange because the rest of us usually follow an opposite procedure. While a child still lives, we do the best that we can for him, trying always to keep our hopes alive. Then, when the child has gone, we give way to our sorrows, our prayers, and our tears. We sense that David's way is more admirable. The man of faith finds the time for sorrow before death, not after.

True enough, the loss of a little one offers many reasons for sorrow. We think of the tragedy of the life cut short, all the potentialities unfulfilled, the object of our love taken from us. The realization of these things calls forth our tears. But David reminds us that such feelings ignore the most important aspects of the situation, the great promises of the faith that we should never forget. For instance, we should never lose sight of the true nature of death from God's point of view. David told us about that when he wrote the words of the shepherd's psalm. (Ps. 23.) Death is not an ending, a disappointment, or a loss of all this world has to offer. Death is a transition, a valley through which we pass with our Lord in order to reach what he has in store for us on the other side. Death is not an ending but an opening of new opportunities, new potentials, which God has prepared for us.

A second thing that David would have us remember is the nature of the God whom we worship. We might have expected to find the old king in rebellion against the God who would not have mercy on him and save his child. On the contrary, the first thing that David did when he heard of the child's death was to go to the House of God to worship. He knew that no matter how things may have seemed at the moment, the Lord was his Shepherd. Jesus came to remind us of the same thing, that God loves us as his children. The cross stands as the reminder of the extent of God's love, a love without limits. God loved us even to the sacrifice of his only begotten Son. (John 3:16.) Then whatever he plans for us or allows to happen to us must be for the best. His love for these little ones must be far greater and far purer than our love. Thus we can trust God to care for them and watch over them no matter what may happen.

75

Finally, we may learn to participate in David's hope. He knew that nothing he did would bring the child back to him again. But his words do not end there. "He will not return to me," he said, "but I shall go to him." Here is an expression of the hope of every Christian. We might think twice about bringing these departed back to be with us, even if we could. Would we force them to return to face the burdens and temptations of life when they have already gone to be in that blessed place in the presence of the living God? Such a plan would ultimately be cruel, and God's provision for us all is far better. The little ones do not return, but we go to be with them. Then once again the family is united, the circle unbroken. Together, in the place God has prepared for us, we greet one another. There we are to spend eternity together in that close fellowship that knows no sorrow, no sin, no misunderstandings, no separation, with our loved ones and with our Heavenly Father.

Almighty God, thy love is far richer and deeper than ours. Help us to trust thee as we prepare to leave this little one in thy keeping. We know not what thou hast planned for him, but our faith tells us that it must be good and right. Comfort us through that faith; for we pray in the name of the Christ, who taught us of thy love. Amen.

15

Christ Loves the Children

Mark 10:13-16

Our Lord had many attractive qualities when he dwelt among us that made him popular wherever he went. One such attribute which is important for us to remember today was his love for little children. He was often busy, but never too busy for them. We can imagine him during his years in the carpenter shop taking time to repair a broken toy for a little girl or to explain to some small lad the tools of his trade. In the short months of his teaching ministry he did not change; the children were always welcome, and he always had time for them.

The disciples were more like the rest of us would have been. They wanted to send the children away. Their own concerns were so important; they did not have the time to be bothered. Children should be seen but not heard, they thought. The little ones were so noisy and dirty, always shouting about unimportant things, the silly affairs that were beneath the dignity of adults. The worst thing of all, the disciples felt, was that parents were actually bringing children to Jesus and asking him to bless them. As if the teacher had nothing better to do than to bother with these boys and girls! If the Master was too polite to tell these people what he thought of such behavior, then his disciples would have to do it for him.

Jesus was not often angry with these close companions of his, but when he saw them turning the children away he was indignant. No one who wanted to see him was ever turned away, children least of all. He turned to his disciples and rebuked them with words that have been repeated over and over until this day. The children were not in the wrong, he indicated. Rather, the disciples should examine their own attitudes. Unless they could become like little children themselves, they could not enter his kingdom. Then he turned his back upon the astounded men, threw his arms around the little street urchins gathered about him, and gave them his blessing.

We must become like little children. He taught us all a lesson in humility with those words. A child is a genuine human being, without art or pretense. He is what he is. He doesn't put on airs as though he were trying to be someone of unusual importance. He knows that he must depend on others for his food, clothing, and shelter. He submits himself in obedience to his father and mother. Thus he judges us adults for our falseness, our pretense. We tend to think we are self-sufficient, and thus we become self-centered. We want others to think we are better and greater than we really are. If we are to be a part of the kingdom of our Lord, we must learn the lesson of humility that these children teach us.

Jesus also reminded us of the necessity of faith when he rebuked his disciples that day. Who is more trusting than a little child? He knows that his parents love him, and he never doubts that love. The sorrows and tragedies of life have not touched him as yet. Thus he feels that life is good, that every problem has its solution, that all things ultimately turn out for the best. He prays at night, "Now I lay me down to sleep; I pray the Lord my soul to keep." In his mind there is not the slightest doubt that God will keep him and care for him. He thinks of his Heavenly Father in terms of his own Daddy, and he cannot doubt. Wasn't this exactly what Jesus had in mind when he told us to address God as "our Father"? But doubts have crowded in upon us. We have experienced temptation and suffering. Our parents have been taken from us by death; our friends have been alienated from us by misunderstandings. We have seen so much tragedy and evil in this world that sometimes we think the whole thing must be twisted and wrong. We tell ourselves that God loves us and that he did not create things to be this way. We remind ourselves of the promises that someday all things will be set right. But, somehow, the world as we know it seems so permanent and so hopeless. We lose ourselves in the problems and responsibilities of the moment, and our faith grows weak. We need to go back to our own childhood days and recapture the faith we once knew, the faith of a little child. If we are to be a part of the kingdom of Christ, we must have such faith.

The obedience of the child is another quality that Jesus must have wanted to emphasize. We parents tend to notice and remember those occasional times of forgetting or of objecting on the part of our children. The fact that we note and remember these events is because they happen so infrequently. Think of the number of instructions we give our children throughout the day, and of how our words guide their actions, their thoughts, and even their attitudes. We adults rebel far more than the children, and some of us are so negative we tend to think or do the opposite of what we are told. Such rebellion against God is the very essence of our sin. Jesus told us that the wise man is the one who hears his words and is obedient to them. (Matt. 7:24.) As far as the commands of God are concerned, we all must become as obedient as little children, always seeking to learn and to follow his will.

So Jesus put out his arms and gathered the children to himself on that day long ago. We assemble today in memory of another member of that throng, a child our Master took to be with himself. We wonder why the Lord would take this one away from us, for we need the child's example for our lives. Yet, we cannot question the wisdom of the decision. We know that the Lord loved, welcomed, and blessed the little children. He has not changed. His will for them must be that which is best, both for them and for those of us who are left behind. Perhaps he wanted this little one to avoid the struggle, pain, and heartbreak of life. Perhaps he had in mind some other field of service for the little one he loves so much. Perhaps he wanted the joy of his fellowship with the other children in that heavenly home. Whatever the reason, we trust his way until that day when we shall have our families reunited.

Our Father in heaven, give each of us the humility, the faith, the obedience of little children. Remind us that thy love for them far exceeds ours, in order that our sorrow at parting might not overcome us. May the blessed memories of the one we have lost for a time serve to comfort and encourage us. We pray in the name of the one who loved and blessed the little children. Amen.

16

On the Death of a Young Man

Luke 7:11-16

Sometimes sorrow follows sorrow in our experience, in an unending drama of misfortune. Just when one family or one individual seems to have endured every possible agony, some new tragedy will take place, and we wonder how they can bear it. It was just such a home that Jesus visited long ago in a city called Nain.

Once this family had been a happy one. The father and mother were united in their love for each other and in their hopes and dreams for their only son. But death came and took the father, leaving the mother and her boy alone. We may imagine how she worked and sacrificed to raise the boy, determined that he would grow into the man she and her husband had hoped to see. As the weeks and months went by and the boy grew tall and strong in the image of her departed husband, her sorrow grew less. He was such a comfort to her, helping around the house and working to supplement their meager income. She was only sorry that his father hadn't lived to know this fine young man who was his son. Then tragedy struck again as the boy became ill and then died. Could anyone be more alone than this poor widow?

Perhaps her friends recognized the extent of her loss, for we read that a great crowd of them assembled to mourn. As the procession carried the body of the lad out of the city to the cemetery, still another group joined them, for they met Jesus and his disciples. This meeting, which almost seems in the record to be by chance, was to make all the difference.

Jesus was always sensitive to sorrow and to human need. He understood the situation immediately. Then he moved to the side of the weeping woman and spoke quietly. "Do not weep," he told her. His words surprise us when we read them, even as they must have surprised the poor widow. Why shouldn't she weep? She certainly had reason enough to be sorrowful. A funeral is an occasion for grief. God does not expect us to conceal our feelings at times like these or to pretend to a false joy that we cannot really experience. Nevertheless, Jesus told her not to weep.

We must admit, however, that Jesus Christ is the only one with the right to make such a command. Only he has the power to turn night to day, to turn sorrow to joy, to turn death into life. What hollow mockery it is for those who have never experienced sorrow to ask the weeping ones to cheer up! What can they know of such problems? But Jesus came to experience sorrow and temptation and even death, and to triumph over them all. He has the right to speak to all of us of joy, even in the midst of our tragedy. If we listen we can hear his voice, even now, speaking to us. "Do not weep. You sorrow because you only understand part of this experience of death. Let me show you something more."

Then Jesus turned and touched the casket. He was not the only one to touch it that day. Loving hands had prepared the body for burial. Others were carrying the casket in the funeral procession. But no one else had touched it in the same way that Jesus did. His was the touch of release, of power. His hand brought the mourning to a halt. He was unique in all that assembly, and the funeral could not continue until he permitted it to do so. His touch had given sight to the blind, hearing to the deaf, cleansing to the leper. Now his touch turned the occasion of sorrow into an occasion of joy, and defeated the power of death itself.

Then Jesus spoke. "Young man, rise up." The dead boy sat up, began to speak, and was restored to the loving arms of his mother. The tragedy had come to an end. Her hopes and dreams were reborn. Tears were replaced by laughter. The resurrection power, of which Christians have spoken so confidently ever since, became a reality to that grieving woman in an instant of time.

That power is still a reality for us today. Our experience of tragedy and loss is still the same. Our tears flow just as easily from sorrow that is just as great. Our ability to find help or comfort in the hour of death is no more than the ability of those people of ancient days. But the Christ is still with us, and we face the time of sorrow in the strength that we receive from faith in him.

He overcomes our grief, for he reminds us that death is not an ending to existence but rather the beginning of a new kind of life. The cross was not the end for him, for on the third day the tomb was empty. He spoke of a place prepared for us after death, the Father's house in which are many rooms. (John 14:2.) Thus we experience the sorrow of parting, but we know we do not part forever, and we look forward to the joy of the reunion.

Our assembly today is thus a gathering of faith and of hope. We have faith in our Lord, who has experienced our sorrows, known our heartbreak and our loss. We have hope in the promises he has given us, that the one who has gone will be restored to us again, and that together we shall be with our Lord in that abode of eternal peace and joy. We hear the Master's voice telling us, "Do not weep." The resurrection power is still among us, and we live in the eager anticipation of that day.

Heavenly Father, thy word reminds us of a Savior stronger than sorrow or death. Help us to trust him as we pass through this difficult experience. Give us of the divine comfort that dries our tears and renews our hope; in the name of Christ our Lord. Amen.

17

On the Loss of a Girl

Mark 5:22-24, 35-43

There was great anxiety in the home of Jairus, one of the rulers of the synagogue. His twelve-year-old daughter was ill and becoming steadily worse. He had called the best physicians, but the doctors offered him no hope. "I have never known one like this to recover," one told him, as he examined the girl. "There is nothing we can do but pray that God will have mercy upon you."

Jairus prayed fervently, but his mind was in turmoil. Surely God would not take his little girl away. But already the news had gone out to friends and relatives, "The doctor says there is no hope." The first wails of the mourners began to rise from the street outside. Still Jairus struggled. Perhaps the doctors were wrong. Perhaps some other physician, wiser and more learned, could do something for his daughter. Then the thought came to him, so powerfully that it seemed almost a specific answer to his prayers: the prophet from Galilee! People had been saying that he could heal the sick. Some even claimed to have seen him do it. Surely, if he could just find this Jesus, he would come and heal his daughter.

The desperate father rushed out of his house and into the streets. In the marketplace he asked everyone he met, "Where is the prophet Jesus of Nazareth? Has he been seen in this part of the country?" In a few moments he had the answer that exceeded his highest hopes. "He's down by the lakeside right now. He crossed the lake by boat and landed only a few minutes ago." Jairus joined the crowds hurrying to the spot where the great healer was to be found.

We are not surprised at these events, even though they happened in a foreign country many centuries ago. The love of father for daughter is not unusual. Serious illness can strike anyone at any time. Medical science has its limitations in our own day. In so many cases the doctor's report must be, "We have done all that we can. There is nothing to do now but to pray and to trust in God." In such an hour many of us turn to Jesus Christ, for he promised to be with us always. (Matt. 28:20.) We feel certain that he has experienced our pain and suffering, that he loves us, that he will do something to help. To whom else would we go in the time of suffering and death?

So Jairus fell at the feet of the Master and begged him, "My little girl is at the point of death. If you will only come and put your hands upon her, I know she will be healed. Hurry now, that she may live." Jesus, of course, consented.

But then events took an unexpected turn. Others had their demands upon the Master also. The crowd got in his way, and progress was slow. A woman stopped him, for she too needed healing. In an agony Jairus waited, not wanting to make demands upon this prophet who might heal his daughter, but at the same time in constant terror that they

87

might be too late. Then he saw a familiar face coming closer in the crowd, and he began to tremble. It was one of his own servants, and Jairus knew what the message must be before he heard it. "Don't trouble the teacher any further. Your daughter is dead."

As far as Jairus was concerned, this word meant the end of everything. He had been too late. His daughter was gone. Nothing that he, the doctor, Jesus, or the weeping friends could do would help now. He turned to go and then noticed that Jesus was still looking at him. "Do not fear," he calmly told the stricken father, "only believe." Together they went to Jairus' house, and Jesus told those weeping there, "There's no need to carry on like this. The girl's not dead but merely asleep."

Those who heard him were astounded. What did he know; he hadn't even seen the girl! How little they understood what he was trying to teach them. To Christ, death was only a sleep. He said the same thing about his friend Lazarus, that he had fallen asleep. (John 11:11.) The apostle Paul learned the lesson, for he wrote of the Christians who had died as having fallen asleep. (I Cor. 15:6.) Let us remember these words in our own moments of grief. This experience of death is nothing more than a sleep. Our Lord will awaken us to a glorious new day in a place prepared for us.

"Do not fear," Jesus told them. "She is not dead but only asleep." This is the Lord's message of hope for all who are in sorrow. We are not afraid of sleep, so why should we be afraid of death? Sleep is God's plan for us, providing rest and recovery from the efforts of the day. We know that it is only a temporary loss of consciousness, that we awake in the morning to the opportunities the new day brings. Death, as Jesus knew it, is just like a sleep, part of God's great plan, a temporary experience marking the transition to a greater day to come.

Jairus could not understand these things until Jesus took him and a few others into the room where the girl lay. Taking her by the hand, he spoke quietly, "Little girl, get up." And as one awakening from a nap, she opened her eyes and looked at him, and immediately she got up.

Jesus' teaching about death was then complete. We sleep for a brief period. Then, at the touch of our Lord, we open our eyes to see his face. We are restored to family and loved ones again, that we might dwell together in happiness in the Father's home.

The miraculous powers that Jesus exercised in the home of Jairus may not literally be ours to use today. We know that in spite of our best efforts, even the fervor of our prayers, the sleep of death awaits all of us eventually. But the lesson that Jesus taught is still true, and it will bring hope and comfort if we will only grasp it. We must not fear in the face of death. The power of God is still with us, the power of the resurrection. In the strength of our faith in him, we know that these who have departed are not dead but asleep.

> There! little girl, don't cry!
>   They have broken your doll, I know;
>   And your tea-set blue,
>   And your play-house, too,
>   Are things of the long ago;

But childish troubles will soon pass by,—
There! little girl, don't cry!

There! little girl, don't cry!
They have broken your slate, I know;
And the glad, wild ways
Of your schoolgirl days
Are things of the long ago;
But life and love will soon come by,—
There! little girl, don't cry!

There! little girl, don't cry!
They have broken your heart, I know;
And the rainbow gleams
Of your youthful dreams
Are things of the long ago;
But Heaven holds all for which you sigh—
There! little girl, don't cry! [1]

Our Father, forgive us our fear in the face of this sleep of death which we cannot understand. Increase our faith, as we look toward the joyful awakening in the morning in thy home. We ask in the name of our Lord, who taught us in word and in deed the reality of the resurrection. Amen.

[1] James Whitcomb Riley, "A Life-Lesson."

18

Treasure in Heaven

Matthew 6:21

As the years pass by, each of us accumulates many things that we treasure. Of course we value our possessions, our property, or our money. We work hard to accumulate these things, and they represent an investment of time and effort. But each of us can also think of other things that we have which we consider of far more than mere commercial value. We remember faded photographs, tiny shoes cast in bronze to preserve them, or the smudges of artwork brought home from school. No one else would offer us cash for these things, and yet hundreds of dollars wouldn't buy them from us.

These objects are only reminders of the greatest treasures of all, our children. How we plan and sacrifice to bring them into the world! How we work that they may have advantages which we never enjoyed! If necessary, we would give all our possessions, even life itself, in order to save one of these little ones.

Sometimes, however, in spite of all that we can do, we are called upon to surrender one of them to death, that great enemy of mankind. No event that could happen to us is more tragic; no loss is more acute. We feel that all that has made life worthwhile has been taken from us. Some may even cry out against God, blaming him for taking away the one whom we hold most dear.

The words of Jesus that we have read, however, give us another point of view. Where our treasures are, there shall our hearts be. The child that we treasured so much is in heaven. Then, in a very real sense, he has not been taken from us at all. A change in relationship has taken place. Now we possess him in a new way, a way we never did before. This new relationship can have a meaning far richer than anything we have known, if we only have the faith to understand it. Where our treasure is, there our hearts will be.

We think of the safety of the treasure that is given into the keeping of the almighty God. On earth, moth or rust could consume or thieves break in and steal. Even our children are not immune from the losses that time and the various events of the world may bring. Misunderstandings may arise and lead to anger and separation, and we lose that which we value most. The passing years or the miles that divide us may diminish the love which was once so important. So often aged parents are completely forgotten by children who are concerned only with their own immediate affairs. Worse still, temptations and sins may come to these young people, alienating them not only from their godly parents but also from their parents' God. In contrast, we think of the little one who has been taken to live in the Father's house, forever removed from misunderstandings and from temptations. He may seem far away, but in truth he is as close to us as God is close. This treasure is in the keeping of our Heavenly Father and cannot be taken from him or from us.

We think also of the inspiration of these treasures of ours who have gone to be with God. The Bible teaches that those who have gone before constitute a cloud of witnesses to our deeds here in the flesh. (Heb. 12:1.) If little son or little daughter watches each deed of ours, we must strive to live in a manner worthy of those watching. We cannot fail them or disappoint them, any more than we could when their tiny eyes watched us in our actions at home. As parents, we know that we are responsible for the moral and spiritual development of our children. Thus we are careful to see that we set them the best examples in all things. The fact that our treasure is now in heaven does not relieve us of this responsibility. Rather, we should be challenged to live on a higher plane than we ever have before. Where our treasure is, our hearts must be, and our deeds must be as heavenly as our affections.

Heaven often seems so far away from us. We are surrounded by material things and constantly busy with everyday activities. We easily forget the unseen world which our faith tells us is the real world. Too often we think of heaven as out beyond the stars somewhere, the place where God lives, an abode we don't bother about until the end of our lives on earth. But now we know that our little one is there, so quickly removed from the family home and taken to dwell in that place which our Lord has prepared for us. Such a short move cannot be to a distant place. One so near to us cannot be regarded as far away. Where our treasure is, our hearts are also, and heaven is now close at hand.

If these treasures of ours may be regarded as nearby, being kept safe for us, then we eagerly anticipate the day when they will be ours once more. The days of separation will be brief, for human life passes quickly. Then comes the time when our Heavenly Father finally brings all the members of his family together. We look forward to the joy of the reunion as husband and wife, brother and sister, parents and children are together again. Our treasures are in heaven, waiting there to greet us on that great day.

Our Father, we surrender that which we loved the most into thy keeping. Let the knowledge of the reality of thy love comfort us in this hour. May heaven seem so close to us now that each thought and each act of ours may be done as in thy presence. Renew our faith as each day passes. Help us to look in hope for the time when we shall be reunited with our loved ones in the kingdom of our Lord; for in his name we pray. Amen.

19

Things That Abide

I Corinthians 13:13

Nothing is permanent in this imperfect world of ours; all things seem to change with the passing years. Most of these changes we expect and accept without difficulty. We replace the appliances in our homes, change jobs, or even move from one place to another. We regard most of these changes as advancements or improvements, and we rejoice at the new opportunities. We are proud of the development of our children, and we measure their progress as they grow taller, advance from grade to grade in school, and finally leave Mother and Dad to establish homes of their own.

Not all these changes are pleasant ones for us. Life brings disappointments and frustrations along with its joys and opportunities. As we grow older, we may increase in wisdom, but our eyes grow dim, hearing is more difficult, and our physical strength gradually departs. The loss of our loved ones, of members of our immediate family, sometimes without warning, is an even more difficult adjustment, but we know that these things happen.

Today, we think of perhaps the most tragic event of all, the death of a young wife and mother. To her husband and to her children, she was the center of the home. They could go out to their various activities of work or school, but Mother was waiting for them at the end of the day. She was always ready with words of sympathy or of advice, offering help when help was needed. But now she is gone. The center of the universe has disappeared, and life itself doesn't seem to make sense anymore.

At such a time, we turn to the Bible in order to seek some understanding and gain some sense of direction. In its pages we discover that our whole understanding of the world, of life and death, has been too limited. We were wrong in thinking that everything changes and that nothing is permanent. The apostle reminds us that some things do not change; there are things that abide. Let us look at them, for they can give us stability in the midst of our sorrow.

First of all, we read that faith abides. We had faith in Mother, that she cared for us and watched over us. We need not give up that faith now that she is gone; she is not far away. Perhaps, in the wisdom of God, she may be given opportunities to see us, even now. The writer of the Hebrew letter spoke of those who were dead as a great group of witnesses, watching our progress in life. (Heb. 12:1.) Mother may even now be numbered in that company.

Mother's faith also abides. She tried to teach her children about a God who loves us and cares for us. Has that faith been proved wrong just because God has taken Mother to be with him? Rather, the opposite is true. Now her faith has been confirmed. While here, she knew only in part. Now she understands everything fully. (I Cor. 13:12.) Her faith is as vital as it ever was; let it strengthen our hearts in these moments. God was and is her Heavenly Father. Let us be confident that he has taken Mother into a life that is far happier, far more wonderful than anything she knew here.

Next, we read that hope abides. Mothers are creatures of hope as they bring children into the world. They know of all the sorrow and temptation that exists. Nevertheless, they nurture their children in hope, in anticipation of the fine men and women they will become. Mother's hope still abides with us. These moments of memory as we gather here should also be a time of rededication to those highest hopes which Mother held for the members of her family.

We are grateful, too, that our hopes are not limited to this life alone. If they were, then as the apostle said, we are most piteous, especially at a time like this. (I Cor. 15:19.) But we have a hope that endures, that extends beyond this experience of death. Our hope is in Christ, and he has been raised from the dead. Thus we can look to that day when in him all shall be made alive. (I Cor. 15:20-22.) We can anticipate that new heaven and new earth in which righteousness will dwell (II Pet. 3:13), and in which all that is wrong or unworthy will be done away.

Finally, we read that love abides. All of us who can remember the experience of Mother's love when we were small should have realized this truth. Not even death can withstand the power of a love so selfless and holy as hers. We remember that when our Lord was dying upon the cross, his mother was there and some of his last thoughts were of her. (John 19:26.) Such love will not end, in the separation of death. You may be sure that Mother's love abides, even now, and is just as real as it ever was.

We must remember that love partakes of the very nature of God himself. (I John 4:7-8.) The love of a mother, which is perhaps the highest and purest of human love, is only a poor approximation of the love of God. He loved us enough to give his only begotten Son to die for us, that we might have eternal life. (John 3:16.) Nothing in all the universe, not even death, can separate us from that love. (Rom. 8:38-39.) Mother's love abides because it is a reflection of this divine love that God has for his children.

As we think of our loving Father in heaven, we remember the promises he has made to us. Death cannot always separate the members of his family. He will bring us together once again, Father, Mother, and the children, reunited in that heavenly home. There the circle of love will once more be complete, never to be broken again. There we shall be forever with our loved ones and with the Lord. With this promise we comfort one another. (I Thess. 4:17-18.)

In the midst of the sorrow of this hour, we need not be fearful or uncertain. Three things still abide, as unchanging as God himself. These three are faith, hope, and love, and the greatest of these is love.

Our Heavenly Father, we look to thee when the very foundations of our lives seem to shake beneath us. In the midst of our uncertainty, remind us of thy unchanging presence. Strengthen our faith, renew our hope. Let thy love dwell within us and comfort us; through Jesus Christ our Lord. Amen.

20

When Death Comes Suddenly

I Samuel 20:3

None of us likes to think about death. We are concerned with life, with our dreams and hopes for the future, with our plans for the days ahead, and with the goals we seek to attain. The end of life seems far away, and death is something that happens to someone else. When one we love comes to the end of his days, we place his tired head upon a silken pillow and close his eyes as if in sleep. Then we surround the casket with flowers as though to distract our attention from the fact of death.

In doing such things, we reveal our human nature. Our faith naturally grows weak in these times of sorrow, and we need these reminders of the true character of death. It is but a sleep, with an awakening in eternity to follow. We are certain that the resurrection power in this universe, represented by these flowers, must be ultimately stronger than the power of the grave.

At other times, death comes suddenly and unexpectedly. In the midst of life, with every joy of living near at hand, the one we love is taken from us. Then we must look squarely into the face of this last great enemy we call death. Then these things that we have done to give comfort seem to mock us. The tragic events of life remind us of the truth of those words uttered by the young man long ago. Death is, indeed, but a step away.

David spoke the literal fact of his own experience. His life was in great danger. The king had turned against him and had tried on more than one occasion to have him killed. There was no hope for him but to hide, and no refuge with his countrymen who were loyal to the king. David's words, however, are just as true for us today as they were three thousand years ago. With all our learning, with all our knowledge of health and disease, with all the precautions we can take, death is still but a step away from any of us. Accidents can happen without warning, as the sad events of the past few days remind us.

Perhaps we can find some comfort in the fact that the step of death is common to us all. Whether the great time-table of God puts death near at hand or far away, it is a step that we all must take. None can escape. Eventually we move into the mysterious land from which no traveler returns. We may be ignorant of the precise moment appointed for each of us, but we are certain, as long as history continues, that the time will arrive.

None of us looks forward to taking that last step, for we know the occasion as a sad one. As we move out into the unknown, we leave our loved ones behind us. We are separated from all that is familiar—the common sights of our everyday lives, the faces of our friends, the voices of those dear to us, the touch of loving hands. Death seems to cut us off from all we hold dear.

Moreover, this final step is one which we must take alone.

All through life we have had others to help us. As children, we were not afraid of the bustle of the big city, for our hands were clasped firmly in the hands of Mother and Father, and we knew we could depend on their love. When we left home to enter school, we discovered that the teacher was there to guide us in these strange surroundings. Over the passing years we have come to know the strength available to us from so many different sources, encouraging us in times of stress. We remember the words of helpful friends, the skills of doctors and nurses, the guidance of a kindly minister. In every crisis, someone was nearby to help. But as we come to the end of life, we face a moment when this help is no longer available. The doctor, the minister, or our friends may be able to comfort and strengthen us until the end comes, but we must take the final step by ourselves.

While these thoughts about death are all true, they are only half-truths. Certainly, death is but a step away from each of us. Disturbing as that fact may be, it is also the source of hope for those of us who anticipate a life beyond.

Death is a step which separates us from those we leave behind, but it is also a step which reunites us with those who have gone before. We remember so many whom we loved in times past and love still though they have long been away. Mother, Father, grandparents, friends—we recall the sad farewell as we followed each one to God's acre. But on the other side of this experience we call death, we know they are waiting for us. Each one is only a step away. Our tearful leaving on this side gives way to the joyous reunion on the other.

Beyond all these human relationships is the love that

101

the Christian knows, tying him to his Lord. The step into eternity is also a step into the presence of Christ. He has gone to prepare a place for us. Then he will receive us unto himself, that where he is we may be also, eternally with our Lord. (John 14:3.)

While the time of death may be uncertain for each of us, there need be no such uncertainty about our destination. The end of life is not marked with a step into the void or into the unknown. We follow in a way that Christ has traveled before us. The eternal home to which we go is far more glorious than our finite minds can comprehend. We only know the depths of love which our Lord expressed to us, and that we shall move into the home that he has prepared. We need nothing more.

As far as human companionship is concerned, we must walk alone in death. However, the Christian has discovered that he has divine fellowship in every moment of life. When he comes to the end and takes that last step, he does not leave God behind. The Shepherd walks always with his sheep. Even when they must walk through the valley of the shadow of death, he does not leave them. They need not fear, for he is present to comfort and to guide. (Ps. 23:4.) Death is but a step away from each of us. Yet, we need not be frightened or anxious. When the time comes, our Father walks with us to the place prepared for us and the heavenly fellowship that awaits us there.

We all know that a journey requires some preparation. If we expect to travel by train or airplane, we buy the tickets, pack the luggage, and make plans to arrive at the depot or airport on time. If we are to drive, we get the automobile ready to carry us to our destination without difficulty.

We would be wise to give some of the same forethought to this last journey which we must take. Death is but a step away. Will you be ready when the time comes?

Our Father, we realize that all of life must be lived in the shadow of eternity. We thank thee for the opportunities that come to us each day to experience thy love and to reflect it toward one another. Forgive us for our failures, and help us to use these days of preparation wisely. Comfort us with thy presence and with the certainty of the hope which thou hast given us; through Jesus Christ our Lord. Amen.

21

It Is Good to Be Here

Matthew 17:1-8

The words that Peter used on the mountaintop have often expressed our own feelings at many pleasant times in life. It is good for us to be here. We remember standing in awe as the rays of the setting sun turned the western sky to flame. We think of moments spent in the company of one deeply loved. We recall some period of achievement and reward when our efforts finally bore fruit, when the long battle was over and the victory was ours. In each case we realized that life is ultimately good, right triumphant over wrong. It is good to be here.

Few of us would hold any such thoughts about the sad occasion which brings us together today. We would avoid a funeral service except for the obligation to pay final respects to one we knew and loved. Life would be much better if it were arranged without any such occasions of mourning at all. How can it possibly be good for us to be here?

Let us turn our thoughts backward across the centuries to that barren Syrian mountaintop on which four weary men spent the night. As we recall some of the things that transformed their surroundings, we may find certain parallels to our meeting here. Perhaps, if we have eyes to see and ears to hear, we can also stand on the mountain of transfiguration and find comfort in our need. For us, as for those apostles long ago, it can be good to be here.

We experience, first, the excitement of a simple Galilean fisherman who suddenly found himself in the presence of Moses and Elijah. From childhood he had been taught the words and deeds of these two men, the lawgiver and the prophet. Now he was able to see them face to face. Both had been dead for centuries, yet both were obviously still living. Each personality was distinct, and each individual the same that Peter knew from his study of the history of his people. These were not shades or ghosts but real men, as much alive as James or John or the Lord himself.

The scholars in Peter's day had long arguments on the subject of life after death. Christ had not yet risen from the grave; and without that central event to guide them, they became lost in a maze of idle speculation. For Peter, however, the issue must have been settled that one night on the mountain. He had seen Moses and Elijah.

We wonder how Peter knew the names of these two whom he had never seen. Jews had strict laws against making images and did not even try to represent the great figures of their past. The record says nothing about Peter being introduced to Moses and Elijah, yet Peter seems to have known exactly who they were. If we have ever wondered about recognizing one another in heaven, we should be reassured by this incident. Not only will we know our loved ones, but we will also recognize individuals of other times and places whom we never had the opportunity of meeting on earth. Our loving Father has provided a future life for us that will surpass our wildest hopes. Sometimes we stand on the mountaintop and catch a little glimpse of what is in store. In the wonder of such a vision, we begin to feel that it is good to be here.

While Peter had no difficulties in identifying his heavenly companions, he also noted some remarkable aspects of their appearance. The change in Jesus must have shocked him the most; he might have expected Moses and Elijah to wear some traces of the heavenly glory from which they had come. But Jesus was the plain carpenter of Nazareth with whom he had walked and talked. Now he witnessed an amazing transformation. Jesus' face was shining like the sun itself, and even his clothes were as white as light. In Christ, God was being made manifest to men; and during those moments on the mountain, Peter, James, and John came as close as human beings can come to looking upon Divinity.

It was good for them to be there and to see such a vision. However, we should keep in mind a further aspect of the Christian faith. When we go to spend eternity with our Lord, we shall see him as he really is. Then we shall make the wonderful discovery that we have been transformed into that same image. The promise is that we shall see him and be like him. (I John 3:1-3.) It was good for Peter to be there to receive a preview of the resurrection body which we are all to be given.

It must have been good for Peter to listen to the conversation that night. Luke tells us that Jesus was talking to Moses and Elijah about his coming departure from Jerusalem, that is to say, about his coming death. We are not surprised at the topic, painful as it must have seemed to Peter. Whenever good friends meet and then leave to go their separate ways, they always speak of their next meeting. Jesus' death would be just such a time, when his earthly mission would be accomplished and he would be able to go back to his Father and those dwelling in his Father's house. The resurrection of our Lord assures us all of this same hope. Death is the time when all of us go to be reunited with our loved ones who have gone before.

Finally, it was good for Peter to listen to the voice of God, even though the words implied a rebuke. Peter sought to put the lawgiver and the prophet on the same level as the Christ. The voice of God pointed out that our Lord is his Son. The law and the prophets have faded into history. Now the world is to be filled with the joyous good news, the gospel. The love of God is stronger than the power of man's sin; we need not perish but can have life everlasting. (John 3:16.) God has adopted us as members of his own family. (Rom. 8:14-17.) We thus look forward to the crown of righteousness which the Lord will award to us when we go to be with him. (II Tim. 4:8.)

As Christians, most of us have learned that it is good to be right where we are, as long as we are serving our Lord. We know that we find contentment in him, even under the most difficult circumstances. (Phil. 4:11.) We do not ignore the sorrow that brings us together here. At such times, however, our minds dwell upon the great promises of the gospel. We think of our coming fellowship with the saints who have gone before us, of the promise of our own resurrection bodies, of the reunion with our Lord. We remember the love of God and the redemption purchased for us by the sacrifice of his Son. In such moments, even the grave can be transfigured, our Christian hope becomes a certainty, and we know that it is good for us to be here.

Our Father in heaven, even in the presence of death we recognize thy loving care over us. Grant us even now the vision that transformed that mountaintop long ago. Remind us again of the certainty of life beyond the grave. Comfort us with the presence of our living Lord. Fill our hearts with the joyous news of thy love for us. Let thy spirit brighten the darkness of our night with the glorious light of thine eternal dawn; through Christ our Lord. Amen.

22

A Conquered Enemy

I Corinthians 15:26

Christianity is a realistic faith. It does not seek to gloss over the difficult or even tragic aspects of life. While it teaches the goodness and the love of God, it admits the evil which is a part of human experience. It confronts man's sin with a Savior nailed to a cross and then points triumphantly to an empty tomb. It even looks courageously at this final experience that we call death, without becoming sentimental or denying the reality of the event. Death is an enemy, and the Christian recognizes the pain, the loss, and the sorrow that it brings. However, the Christian is sustained by the promise of the ultimate defeat of this enemy, for he knows that the last enemy to be destroyed is death.

Some doctrines of the Christian faith may be difficult for us to understand, but we have no such problem with this view of death. We have seen the face of the enemy too frequently. We have known death as the great destroyer, silencing the pen of the poet and the voice of the orator. Death has taken away our national leaders at times when their wisdom seemed most needed by their country. Our most brilliant intellects have been taken on the eve of their most significant contributions. Artists have dropped their brushes and musicians their instruments at the call of death. We wonder what the genius of Mozart or Schubert would have produced had a few more years of life been granted them. What would Lincoln or Franklin Roosevelt or Kennedy have meant to America if they had had only a few months longer to serve? We think of our young men who have stained the battlefields of the world with their blood. How much more they could have accomplished but for the sudden death which overtook them!

We have seen the sorrow that death can bring to our loved ones and to ourselves. Parents have had their hopes and dreams destroyed when a little child was taken from them. Young people have been forced to grow to maturity without the love and guidance of father or mother. Husband has been separated from wife, brother from sister, friend from friend by the power of death. Our efforts to withstand the attack of this enemy have only gained a little delay; eventually death triumphs over all of us. Of all the enemies that confront mankind, death must surely be the greatest.

However, a strange fact of life is that enemies sometimes change into friends. We have seen such shifts take place so often in the tangled relationships among nations. We fought against England in 1812, but a hundred years later, in 1917, we came to her aid. Spain was our enemy at the turn of the century; fifty years later she was letting us construct air bases on her soil. Relationships between individuals can change even faster. Let the issue be joined, the conflict brought to a head, the decision reached, and old animosities may disappear. Those who formerly hated each other become the best of friends.

The Christian view of death may be understood in terms such as these. While death is the last enemy to be destroyed, that destruction began with the resurrection of our Lord. He was the "firstfruits" of those who are to be raised from the grave. As human beings, the descendants of Adam, we are all to die, but in Christ we are all to be made alive. (I Cor. 15:22-23.) Our Lord was victorious in a battle fought two thousand years ago when it proved impossible for death to hold him. (Acts 2:24.) Now he lives and reigns; death has no dominion over him. (Rom. 6:9.) We live in the joyous reality of that victory.

Christ counteracts the powers of death at every point. Where death is the great destroyer, bringing an end to life, our Lord is the supreme life giver. He spoke of himself as the bread of life (John 6:35), and as the source of living water. (John 4:14.) He offered himself to his followers as the way, the truth, and the life. (John 14:6.) His very purpose in coming was that we might have life and have it more abundantly. (John 10:10.)

Where death brings separation, Christ reunites. He went to visit the home of his friends in Bethany where two sisters mourned the loss of their brother. "I am the resurrection, and the life," he reminded them. (John 11:25.) Then he called Lazarus from the tomb, and the family was united once again. He taught us that he has gone to prepare a place for us. We all anticipate the day when we will be with him, reunited with our loved ones in the Father's house. (John 14:3.)

Where death brings sorrow, Christ brings joy. He enables us to look beyond the pain and suffering of this life to the wonderful existence that will be ours in eternity. Our finite minds cannot grasp the life beyond, for it is unlike anything we know, and we have nothing with which to compare it. However, we are promised that some of the things we have experienced here will no longer be part of our lives there. Mourning, crying, and pain will forever be eliminated. (Rev. 21:4.) Hunger, thirst, and scorching heat shall be no more. (Rev. 7:16.) Ours will be the everlasting joy of service to God and of fellowship with him.

The last enemy to be destroyed is death, but in Christ the victory is already ours. As Christians, then, we need no longer regard death as an enemy. For us, death means rest from our labor, surcease from pain, and an access into the very presence of God. In the face of death we can raise the triumphant cry, "Thanks be to God who gives us the victory through our Lord Jesus Christ." (I Cor. 15:57.)

Our Father, in the midst of our sorrow and defeat we would hear again that triumphant shout, "The kingdoms of this world have become the kingdoms of our Lord and of his Christ, and he shall reign for ever and ever." Help us to find comfort in the certainty of this victory. Give us the faith to live each moment of each day in the assurance of our Christian hope; for we pray in Jesus' name. Amen.

23

Death Is Gain

Philippians 1:21

How shall we summarize the life of the departed? The words of the obituary are certainly inadequate. Such a brief list of facts conveys nothing of the real personality that has gone. Even the fond memories of those left behind are too fragmentary to express the full impact of the one we knew and loved. Only God can pronounce final judgment, and perhaps the only human words worthy of notice are those expressing the conclusions each of us reaches about his own life.

Our scripture reading is just such a summary, the words of the apostle Paul as he looked back over his own experiences. As he sat in prison, awaiting his trial, he courageously faced the two alternatives open before him and gave his reaction to them both. Whether living or dead, his only desire was to honor Christ. If he lived, Christ would live in him. If he died, he would gain.

We marvel at a life so consecrated, yet we know that Paul was expressing the goal of every Christian. We all try to live after the example of our Lord. We would exhibit his patience in suffering, his virtue in temptation, his faith in moments of uncertainty, and his love in all our relationships. The apostle, in one of his letters, recounted some of the persecutions he had experienced. He had been beaten with the lash five times, with rods three times, stoned almost to death once, shipwrecked three times, and had lived in constant danger. (II Cor. 11:24-26.) All such suffering was merely a poor imitation of the example of his Lord, who had been obedient unto death, even the death of the cross. (Phil. 2:8.) When Paul was thrust into prison, he never forgot his Christian obligations. He used the opportunity to preach to his own guards and set an example which was an encouragement to all his friends. (Phil. 1:12-14.) Paul's aim was to live like Christ.

For us to live is for Christ to live. These words remind us not only of our future goals but also of our past experiences. As Christians of every age will testify, our Lord has been our constant companion, even in dangerous and difficult times. As Paul remembered the hardships he had undergone, he also thought of the unfailing strength he had received. Years before, on the road to Damascus, he had chosen to surrender himself to the authority of Christ. As he later wrote, he had been crucified with Christ, and it was no longer he that lived. Christ lived in him. Each day that passed was lived in faith in the Son of God. (Gal. 2:20.) For Paul to live was for Christ to live, and the Lord who had accompanied him through life would also be with him in death. To die would be gain.

Such a faith is difficult for us to grasp, for we regard death as the ultimate misfortune, the final tragedy. We reserve it as punishment for the most serious crimes and seek to avoid it with all our knowledge and skill. Paul, however, looked at death from the vantage point of his triumphant life and his Christian faith. He knew that this event marked the point of transition to all the rewards that would be his. Thus to die is gain.

Paul must have looked forward to the new body that he would receive in the life to come. As he grasped the bars of his cell and as he felt the chafing of the chains on his wrists, how he must have longed for the freedom that death would bring! He spoke the literal truth when he pointed out that the marks of Jesus were upon his body. (Gal. 6:17.) The scars of his beatings were obvious. Then Paul had another physical affliction which he called a "thorn in the flesh." He never identified this handicap in his letters, but he thought of it as a "messenger of Satan" and made it the subject of much fervent prayer. (II Cor. 12:7-8.) Is it any wonder that he looked to the future with such eager anticipation? He was certain that when this earthly dwelling place, this mortal body, had gone back to dust, he would live on in a building not made with hands, an immortal body which God would give him. (II Cor. 5:1.)

The Christian lives in the hope of this same transformation. Our bodies are placed in the ground in all their weakness and mortality; they are raised into a new kind of existence, changed and renewed. The perishable becomes imperishable, the dishonorable becomes glorious, and the physical becomes spiritual. (I Cor. 15:42-44.) The mortal puts on immortality. (I Cor. 15:54.) We know not what these new bodies of ours will be like except to say that we shall be like our Lord, for we shall see him as he is. (I John 3:2.) In death, we gain new bodies.

Paul also expected a new home beyond the grave; he had

115

known so little of home in this life! Today we trace his wanderings over most of the civilized world of his time. He never stayed long in one place, for his ears always caught the call of some new district needing the gospel of Christ. "Come over into Macedonia and help us," was the plea on every hand. (Acts 16:9.) So he went, to Cyprus and Asia Minor, to Greece and on to Rome. At the end, his home was a prison cell from which only death could deliver him. Yet in this respect he was also no different from his Lord, who had nowhere to lay his head. (Matt. 8:20.)

The man of faith can never be completely at home in this world. He is a citizen of another country and only lives here as a stranger and exile. Thus we look forward to a heavenly city which God has prepared for us. (Heb. 11:13-16.) Our Lord promised us a home, a room in his Father's house. (John 14:2-3.) We live in expectation of the family reunion that awaits us, the gathering of the children of God, when we greet our loved ones once again and the broken fellowship is renewed, when the sorrow of parting is forever forgotten. In death, we gain a new home.

As Paul thought of the advantages of the life to come over his existence here, he often wished that the end would come. He would much prefer to depart and be with Christ. Yet he knew that a task remained for him on earth and that he could not move on until his work was completed. It was necessary for him to stay for the sake of those he could serve. (Phil. 1:24.) Nevertheless, he knew that death would bring gain even in this respect. If we endure, we are to reign with Christ. (II Tim. 2:12.) Newer and far greater avenues of service will be opened to us.

We think of heaven as a place of rest, and so it is. Our

heavenly rest, however, is not to be idleness. When we have finished our brief period of preparation here, God takes us to himself that our true mission might be fulfilled over there. We do not know what tasks God has planned for us. We may be sure, however, that the joys we have known in serving him here will be nothing in comparison with the joy he has in store for us there. Perhaps we can find no better description than the one given us by the writer of the Revelation, that God shall be our light, and we will reign with him for ever and ever. (Rev. 22:5.)

How shall we summarize the life of the departed? Each Christian is entitled to use the words of the apostle. For me to live is Christ. To die is gain.

Almighty God, we bow in humility before thee, for our sin is ever before us and we know the bitterness of our failure to follow the example Jesus set for us. We thank thee that he came not to judge us but to show us thy love and mercy. In this hour of our sorrow and our need, we would dedicate ourselves anew to our Lord, that through faith we might share in his righteousness. Let his presence within us bring us comfort and hope, even in times like these; for in his name we pray. Amen.

24

Additional Outlines of Funeral Meditations

Blessed Mourners (Matt. 5:4)

The mourners are blessed, for they are to be comforted.
1. They are to be comforted by the Lord, who sends the Comforter (John 14:16).
2. They are to be comforted by one another, for giving such comfort is our Christian responsibility (I Thess. 4:18).
3. They are to be comforted by the promise or hope of a brighter future (Rev. 21:4).

Some Things We Know

There are many things that we do not know and cannot know. It is impossible for us to know the future. Neither can we know about events and places too far removed from us. But there are some things which we may know because God has revealed them to us.
1. We know of the certainty of death (Heb. 9:27a).
2. We know that death cannot separate us from God's love (Rom. 8:38).

118

3. We know that ultimately all things work together for good (Rom. 8:28).
4. If these bodies which we inhabit be destroyed, we go to dwell in heavenly buildings (II Cor. 5:1).
5. Then, we shall be like Christ (I John 3:2).

A Happy Farewell (II Tim. 4:8)

Paul thought of death in many ways, but he regarded his own death as a departure. He must have experienced many such moments in his travels (*e.g.* Acts 20:36-38). We also often face the moment of farewell. But when that moment came, Paul was ready to go.

1. He had completed his task, having finished the course of life laid out for him and having kept the faith entrusted to him.
2. He knew where he was going—to see the Lord, the righteous Judge.
3. He knew the award waiting for him there—the crown of righteousness.

Seeing the Unseen (II Cor. 4:18)

We appreciate the beauties of nature and much of what we see around us in this world. However, in the time of death we must learn to see the unseen. That which we see is often temporary; the unseen is the eternal.

1. The aspects of nature that we can observe are constantly changing and passing away. The creative power of God in nature is eternal.
2. The Bible is only paper and print. The word of God will stand forever (Isa. 40:8).

3. Local churches consist of fallible humans. The church cannot be overcome (Matt. 16:18).
4. Our dwelling places crumble and decay. God gives us a house not made with hands (II Cor. 5:1).
5. Our physical bodies deteriorate and die. The resurrection means that we put on immortality (I Cor. 15:53-54).

The Light of the World (John 8:12)

Light has many functions. We think of the traffic lights, or of the headlights on an automobile or train. We remember the beautiful lights that decorate a Christmas tree. One of the main functions of light in our existence is to reveal. Without light we would be completely unable to see the things around us. So Christ is the light which reveals.

1. He reveals God.
   Man has ever tried to find God. Philip promised that he would be satisfied if he could only see the Father. Jesus answered that the one who had seen him had seen the Father (John 14:8-9). Christ revealed God as the loving Father.
2. He reveals man.
   He saw man as precious in the sight of God (John 3:16).
3. He reveals life beyond the grave (John 11:25).
4. He reveals heaven and the way there (John 14:2, 6).

The Death of the Righteous (Num. 23:10)

We must all die, the righteous and the unrighteous. All of us desire, along with the prophet of old, to die the death of the righteous. We want to face eternity in hope, with comfort for those left behind. Let us note some of the characteristics of these righteous.

1. They have been led in the right paths (Ps. 23:3). The Lord led them, but let us give thanks for the godly parents, teachers, and friends whom he used.
2. They have hope in death (Prov. 14:32, alternate reading). This hope can live in the presence of personal pain and suffering (Job 19:25-27).
3. They have faith in Christ (Phil. 3:9-11). They find their righteousness in him. Thus they have the certainty of the resurrection through his power (Phil. 3:21).

Rest for the Weary (Matt. 11:28)

1. All of us become weary and long for rest.
   The problems of life overtake us. Like David we would like to leave everything behind and find peace (Ps. 55:6). Perhaps David thought of those green pastures in which he had found rest for his sheep (Ps. 23:2). He longed for God to give him rest like that.
2. We find this rest in Christ.
   In this life he helps us with our burdens.
   He gives us the assurance of rest in the life to come (Heb. 4:9-11).

Thus we can find meaning and hope in the experience that we call death (Rev. 14:13).

Happy Are the Dead (Rev. 14:13)

We think of death as the time of sorrow, and so it is for those who lose a loved one. For the child of God, however, who goes to be with his Father, it is a time of joy. The

Scriptures teach that those who die in the Lord are blessed or happy. We should not be surprised that it is so.

1. They are happy because they are with the Lord.

    They have known the fellowship with God's people here and the joy of the Christian life (Matt. 5:1-12). Now they experience the richer fellowship beyond the grave, a fellowship with Christ himself (John 14:3; II Cor. 5:8).

2. They are happy because of the place they are in.

    It is a place prepared for them (John 14:2).

    It is a place of joy (Rev. 7:16-17; 21:1-4).

3. They are happy because they rest.

    The Lord has given them rest in this life (Matt. 11:28).

    He promises a greater rest in the life to come (Heb. 4:9-10).

4. They are happy because of their works.

    Their wrongdoing has been forgiven and forgotten, even by God (Jer. 31:34).

    Now they receive their reward (II Tim. 4:8).

The Salt of the Earth (Matt. 5:13)

We often use the expression "the salt of the earth" to refer to individuals who embody true greatness no matter what their station in life might have been. Jesus used the term for common, humble people who were obedient to the will of God. His striking figure reminds us of certain characteristics of such people:

1. They assist in the cleansing of their environment.

    As salt is an antiseptic agent, so these people participate in the eradication of evil from society.

    In doing so, they are true children of their Heavenly

Father. He is the author of all cleansing, for sin is primarily against God (Luke 15:21) and only he can offer ultimate forgiveness (Mark 2:7).

However, we can help to mediate the divine forgiveness (Jas. 5:15, 20; II Cor. 5:19).

2. They assist in the preservation of all that is best.

Evil is always self-destructive and could not exist alone; it is a parasite which feeds off the good. Were it not for the righteous, preserving society, everything would be chaos.

Again, they are children of their Father, for his power brings order in the universe (Col. 1:17).

By embodying this divine power, these people are both salt and light to the world (Matt. 5:14).

Without them the very social structure could not be preserved (Ezek. 22:30).

3. They continue to live when all else disappears.

The salt which preserves must partake of eternal qualities.

Having the divine nature, these people participate in a hope reaching beyond this life (Col. 3:3-4).

Thus the grave holds no fears for them (I Cor. 15: 54-57).

They anticipate the reward beyond (II Tim. 4:8).

The Bread of Life (John 6:57-58)

We think of bread as the staff of life. It represents the powers of the universe, the sun, rain, and soil which we appropriate that we might live. The Christian faith is grounded in a similar understanding of our Lord as the bread of life.

1. He appropriates the power of the universe for us.

   He was sent by the Father, the source of all life (John 20:21).

   God's creative power was in him (John 1:3).

2. He makes God's power available to us.

   No one has seen God, but the Son makes him known (John 1:18).

   He shows God to us (John 1:14; Col. 2:9).

   Even our sin is not a barrier to finding God in Christ (Rom. 5:8).

   So just as the grain means life to all who partake, so Christ makes eternal life available to all (John 1:12).

3. The divine power brings eternal hope.

   Just as the grain enters the very cells of our bodies to strengthen us, so our Lord becomes a part of our being (John 6:51).

   This power within brings us the assurance of life beyond the grave (John 6:40).

   The bread of life produces new, eternal bodies (I Cor. 15:53). Therefore, let us not sorrow but rather give thanks (I Cor. 15:57).

The Water of Life (John 4:14)

The ancient Spanish explorers sought for a fountain of youth, and we have never given up hope. We try everything to preserve the health and vitality of youth and, failing that, to preserve the appearance of youth. Nevertheless, the grave marks our ultimate failure. Over against our need, Christ proclaims his adequacy. He comes to us as the water of life.

1. Water speaks of cleansing.

Water is the great cleansing agent.

Jesus spoke of the worship of God in spirit and truth to a woman whose whole life was falsehood and sin (John 4:16-24).

His whole purpose was not to condemn us but to save us (John 3:17).

2. Water speaks of power.

Much of our physical power comes from waterfalls or from gigantic dams.

So Christ gives us power:

To become sons of God (John 1:12).

To live victoriously (Rom. 7:25).

To overcome our weakness (Rom. 8:26).

3. Water speaks of fertility.

Given water, the desert blooms like a rose.

So in Christ, man can develop his full potential. He is freed from sin (Rom. 6:22) and brought into obedient relationship with God. His life is given meaning and purpose. Thus he achieves satisfaction, a spring of living water (John 4:14).

4. Water speaks of renewal.

As water goes through its endless cycle, descending from heaven, doing its work, then drawn up again by the sun to continue its service elsewhere; so our potential is never realized in this life. We are lifted through the power of God's Son to a greater life beyond (I John 3:2).

The Father Knows (II Cor. 5:11)

We never really know one another. Even the closest human relationships, parents-children, husband-wife, brothers-sisters, never involve complete understanding. Only God truly knows us, and in this knowledge we find comfort.

1. We are freed from any need to pretend (II Cor. 5:17).

   God knows what we are and accepts us in spite of it (II Cor. 5:19; Rom. 5:8).

   He gives us new natures. The old is forgotten (Jer. 31:34).

   God knows us for what we are in Christ.

2. We are given courage (II Cor. 5:6).

   Through constant renewal in our need (II Cor. 4:16-17).

   Our fear of death is past (II Cor. 5:14).

   Our faith enables us to walk ahead (II Cor. 5:7; Ps. 23:4).

   The Spirit within us is our assurance (II Cor. 5:5).

3. We are given hope (II Cor. 4:17–5:1).

   Of a future that is glorious (II Cor. 4:17).

   Of a future that is eternal (II Cor. 4:18).

   Of a future prepared by our loving Father (II Cor. 5:1).

   Of a future in our heavenly home (II Cor. 5:7-8).

So we are not troubled, but trust our Lord even in the time of death (John 14:1-3).

The Life Complete (Col. 2:9-10)

We sometimes think of death as marking the end of life. We are self-centered, and we regard those who have passed beyond our sight as having passed out of existence. At other times we think more deeply in the light of our Christian faith and remember that death is only an incident in the pattern of development planned for us by our Heavenly Father. Life could never be completed in death, for this experience often cuts across life at a time that is most inappropriate, when life is least complete. The true fullness or completeness of life is found in Christ and has nothing to do with the experience of death at all. Finding the complete life in Christ involves three things:

1. The admission of our own incompleteness.
   Our lives are out of balance when seen from the standpoint of time. Death appears victorious in the end.
   Our days seem to be purposeless and lonely.
   We are helpless to complete life (Rom. 5:6).
2. An understanding of God's plan for us.
   From the standpoint of eternity, life is in balance again; life is triumphant over death (I Cor. 15:55).
   Thus life has direction and purpose. We are never alone (Matt. 28:20).
3. The realization that life can be complete now.
   We are victorious over trials and sorrows (Rom. 8:28).
   Life has purpose and direction (Rom. 8:30).
   We receive strength for our weakness (Rom. 8:26).
   Our ultimate triumph is certain (Rom. 8:37-39).

Since our lives are now complete, we need not be fearful or sorrowful in the face of death. We see, rather, the glory of eternity toward which we grow (Rom. 8:16-17).

The Blessed Man (Ps. 1:1-3)

Certain evergreen trees are among the oldest living things on earth. All of us have seen their cross sections, with the size of the tree marked for 1066, 1492, 1776, and all the famous dates of history. How we wish we might partake of this same eternal quality! The message of the psalmist is that we can, and he tells us why.

127

1. We can be eternal in our living (Ps. 1:1).

   Certain habits of life are self-destructive. The man who can live above these things begins to partake of eternal life.

2. We can be eternal in our thinking (Ps. 1:2).

   We tend to resemble whatever catches our full attention, like young Ernest in Hawthorne's *Great Stone Face*. As we center our lives on things above, we partake of eternal life.

3. We can be eternal in our influence (Ps. 1:3).

   The tree yields fruit in season. These influences of our lives are not from us at all, but from the Spirit of God within us (Gal. 5:22-23). Hence they are eternal.

Thus we face the moment of death in confidence. The Lord knows the way of the righteous (Ps. 1:6). We partake of his nature, and we need have no fear of what the future holds for us.